THINKING RUGBY

THINKING RUGBY

the London Welsh way

GEOFF EVANS, DENIS HORGAN
and GARETH JAMES
Edited by JOHN DAWES

London
GEORGE ALLEN & UNWIN
Boston   Sydney

First published in 1979

GEORGE ALLEN & UNWIN
40 Museum Street, London, WC1A 1LU.

British Library Cataloguing in Publication Data

Evans, Geoff
  Thinking Rugby.
  1. Rugby football coaching
  I. Title   II. Horgan, Denis
  III. James, Gareth
  796.33′3′077   GV945.75   78-40697

  ISBN 0–04–796051–5

Typeset in 11 on 12 point Times Roman
and printed in Great Britain
by Hazell Watson and Viney Ltd, Aylesbury, Bucks.

Contents

Photographs

Diagrams

NB. The following symbols are used in the diagrams:

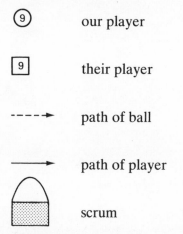

(9) our player

[9] their player

----▶ path of ball

——▶ path of player

scrum

xiv

Editor's Preface

There have been quite a few books written about the technical aspects of rugby football, but most of the better ones have been written by people whose knowledge and tactical appreciation of the game has been gained through years of study and application throughout the world of rugby football. What is refreshing about this book is that it is written by three people who have seen their thoughts and their philosophies realised in a very positive and enjoyable way. Denis Horgan, Geoff Evans and Gareth James were among the several forceful personalities who were responsible for the truly magnificent period in London Welsh's history when they gained national – almost world-wide – recognition for their particular brand of positive, enjoyable, thinking rugby.

Of course London Welsh were blessed with gifted players during this spell, but what must be realised is that it was the philosophy and style of play within the club which made these players realise their full potential. The authors have tried to write down and explain, for the benefit of other players, what made it all happen and how valuable the contribution of the individual is within the framework of a team or club.

One of the remarkable features of this book is that originally each author wrote independently, yet there are so many common factors that their contributions fuse into a very readable whole, answering the questions with which players are confronted and yet quite clearly emphasising that every player is a decision-maker and must not shun that responsibility.

The book also emphasises, quite correctly, the basics of the game – no book about coaching could really fail to do so – but it goes beyond even that. The point comes over quite clearly that, whilst execution of the basic ploys is essential, there is much more to do and think about. The game is a continual challenge all about trying to outwit your opponents, eliminating mistakes but maintaining that element of surprise and decision-making that brings the unexpected. Whilst tactical appreciation is assuming greater importance in modern rugby and this book emphasises that need, it is so encouraging to read that the perceptions and ability of the individual are a dominant factor and must be exploited. It is no good having talented players if the system or the approach or the style of play eliminates all such flair. This is an attempt to illustrate to players that the correct balance can be found, with the result that the game can be a spectacle and still have the modern objectives of success and enjoyment.

Since London Welsh may be typical of many rugby clubs, the early chapters give a brief insight into the structure of the club as well as indicating the philosophy and policy of the club itself. Every club needs its administrators and daily workers, but these early pages show that the playing of the game is, and must be, the paramount objective. It illustrates that the whole structure of a club is built around the playing side and that in return the players are allowed a freedom of expression which manifests itself during the game itself. Great care and thought is given to the organisation of training, the number of games in a season, the demands on the players whether social, domestic or business – even travel problems. Each player is treated as an individual and every effort is made to develop his ability to the full and make him feel a valuable contributing member of team and club.

The middle chapters deal with those specific skills needed for particular positions or units. Whilst one might say it has all been written before, here it is explained simply and obviously by people who know through personal experience the problems of these positions. The importance of these basics is emphasised, and rightly so, but what is refreshing and seldom seen in print is that the game demands much more. It is practice and organisation which improves the ball winning capacity of a team but it is the approach and the confidence to attempt something adventurous which makes the game so enjoyable and worthwhile.

The latter part of the book is full of suggestions, many of which may be known to the players, but over and over again the point is made that there is room in the game for the unplanned move, the flair of the individual and the positive approach.

The book is an attempt to illustrate that with application, organisation, individualism, confidence and right attitude the game of rugby football offers to the player enjoyment and satisfaction that no other sport can better. If a criticism of the book is that it makes it seem too simple and that it is not as easy as suggested, then I for one can refute it. The reason for such a statement is simple – everything written here has worked. I know because I played in it.

JOHN DAWES

1

Strategy and Tactics

DEFINITION

Strategy in rugby football, the art of employing basic skills to gain fair advantage over your opponents during a game, is the key to a successful side. A team's strategy must be planned for each season, each coaching session and each game. It forms the plan of a game, maps out its proposed course and regulates its competitive tempo. The higher the level of competition the more planning and coaching should go into preparing the strategy.

Tactics, on the other hand, is the organisation and execution of skills during a game; it is the means by which the strategy is deployed. It may be defined as the ability to assess the relative strengths and weaknesses of your team and the opposition, both before and during a match, and to adjust your play to any situation with the ability at your disposal. Tactics are not merely, as some people might think, the learning of numerous skills or techniques, set ploys or moves, with the sole intention of reeling them off during a game and expecting them to produce a winning result every time. They are more complex than that: a player may be technically a fine runner, passer or kicker but invariably choose the wrong option through lack of tactical judgement, or a team loses games against less skilful sides by choosing and sticking to wrong tactics.

IMPORTANCE OF A GAME PLAN

Any team taking the field and simply trying to attack the

opposition without any plan or system of ideas will soon come to grief. One time in a hundred, the more disorganised and disjointed side might come out winners, but rugby football today is a highly coached game. In the last decade it has become so much more organised that not only first class, but second and even third class rugby clubs are taking their games more seriously. Leagues and cup competitions give an incentive for success and recognition at all levels, so clubs throughout the country are looking more closely not only at their own standard of play but at that of their opposition as well.

The game is more deeply analysed, many more coaching books and manuals are being written, more detailed and concentrated coaching courses are available. The exploits of the British Lions during the early 1970s improved the status of British rugby in the world game and placed a greater emphasis on rugby success than ever before. More schools have added rugby to their curriculum, while the now familiar mini-rugby has meant not only that boys are learning the basics of the game at a far younger age, but also that rugby clubs all over the country should in time reap the benefits of the work they are putting in with their youngsters.

WHO DECIDES THE STRATEGY AND TACTICS?

Is it the coach who has charge of the team off the field of play or is it the captain who has the responsibility on the field? Does it extend even to each individual player? The answer is of course a combination of all three. The coach and captain must always work in close contact with each other, continually exchanging ideas and working towards the same end of what will prove best for their team. However, once on the field of play, it falls to each individual player to carry out the strategy and tactics determined by the coach or captain.

2

The Playing Organisation

THE IMPORTANCE OF GOOD ORGANISATION

Bearing in mind the remarks in the previous chapter, it is easy to see that a rugby club must be a highly organised unit on and off the field. There is indeed a very close relationship between tactics and organisation and the following is an example of the organisation of the playing side of one club (London Welsh) which has been found to work well. It should not, however, be taken as gospel, and will need to be adapted to individual circumstances.

Mini-rugby
Under-8, under-9, under-10, under-11. The aims are:

1. To introduce youngsters to the game and the club.
2. To involve every individual in enjoyable activity connected with the game, so that they want to continue playing.
3. To teach as many skills and techniques as possible within the limitations of mini-rugby.
4. To teach all those participating, players and spectators, to adopt the correct attitudes and behaviour on and off the field of play.
5. To provide a limited amount of competition by playing sides from other clubs.
6. To provide adults with the opportunity of gaining coaching experience.

Schoolboy fifteen-a-side
Under-14, under-16, under-19. The aims are:

1. As for mini-rugby.
2. To set up a form of communication with school and county organisations in the area. The club insists that players' loyalty is to school, county and then club, in that order, although in the future a greater responsibility for developing players may rest on the clubs.
3. To develop the coaching process so that all players have the opportunity of improving individual skills and techniques.
4. To groom players for senior rugby.
5. To encourage the boys to attend WRU and RFU coaching courses.
6. To provide adults with the opportunity of doing more advanced coaching with a view to progressing to the coaching of senior sides.

Junior sides
4th XV, 5th XV, 6th XV, 7th XV. The aims are:

1. As for schoolboy rugby.
2. To cater for the needs of the schoolboy players as they become available and to provide members of the club with the opportunity of an organised game of rugby.
3. To provide a means whereby the best players may challenge for a place in the senior sides.

Senior sides
1st XV, 2nd XV, 3rd XV. The aims are:

1. As for junior sides.
2. To provide coaching which will give the first-class player the opportunity to reach his peak performance as an individual, part of the unit and part of the team.
3. To win as many games as possible in the season.

4. To produce the best 1st XV available.
5. To provide an opportunity for players to gain representative honours.

THE SQUAD SYSTEM

If a club has several teams it naturally has a greater depth of playing ability than a club with one or two sides, but it does mean also a greater range of talent. Each team's style of play will be different, although they all belong to the same club, and this is where the system of squad training comes in. A club which has six or more teams should set up separate squads, each consisting of a combination of two or three teams, ideally each with its own coach but under the overall guidance of the club coach. Whether they train at different times or all together depends entirely on club policy and on the facilities available. The senior squad should of course be flexible enough to allow the introduction of players who have improved their standard of play in the lower teams.

If a club has only one, two or three teams there need only be one squad and one club coach, with assistant specialist coaches to help if they are available. The great advantage of the squad system, of course, is that if selection of a team changes from week to week, each player knows his own particular role in the team plan.

Optimum size

A squad should consist of thirty players, two full teams, although forty-five players, three teams, is acceptable. A three-team squad has the advantages of bringing together more players at one time and of making it easier to fill in at training sessions for people unable to attend, but its effectiveness is limited by the number of coaches, and it can mean more standing around and possible wasting of time at a session. Clubs usually start by running one or two teams (the majority of Welsh clubs, for example) and have a squad of around thirty players.

The rota system

If a squad consists of twenty-five players or less it should mean that the club has probably only one team. As is the case in Wales, the facility of floodlit pitches means mid-week as well as weekend fixtures, and therefore a large fixture list. In this case a rota system, whereby players are rested and replaced by other members of the squad, can be used. Players are still quite happily involved in a great many matches during the season, and they benefit physically, avoiding excessive demands on their fitness. A rota system also solves the problem of players who are completely inseparable in talent and ability, both being of equal use to the team.

A squad consisting of thirty or more players would probably mean that a club has two or more teams and in this case a rota system may not be necessary. Both or all teams making up the squad would receive coaching and training together but would probably play as their own separate teams. Changes would take place only because of loss or improvement of form, injury or unavailability. However, if certain players are considered to be equal in ability even here a rota system may be used.

The squad system should mean that any member of a squad is automatically considered capable and talented enough to play in a selected team taken from that squad. It is at squad sessions that strategy and pre-match tactics are evolved and practised.

3

Coaching

In recent years, changes in the laws and the improvement in playing techniques have made rugby football a much more open and attacking game. The value of coaching has been universally acclaimed and accepted, and players are working to become much fitter and technically more efficient. Good team-work is based upon sound organisation and method but this method is in turn based upon a solid framework of skilful individuals, for however well organised a team may be, it is dependent upon the individuals which make it up. Coaching aims to stimulate, enthuse and educate the players so that they will improve their performances and thereby that of the team. It aims to help the team to realise its full collective potential by providing a framework of method and organisation within which the individual players can express themselves in a confident and positive way on the field of play.

THE CLUB COACH

These days a club should ideally appoint a club coach so that the responsibility for the organisation of the playing side, ie. the teams taking the field, falls squarely on one person's shoulders. As the coach should not have been selected if unsuitable or unable to take this on, it is not an unfair responsibility, although obviously he should not be left completely out on a limb, and any advice or help he wants should be given by the club. His main duties are organisation of the coaching and training plan, coaching the teams themselves, selecting or helping to select the teams, and finally preparing pre-match tactics.

Rugby is a decision-making game. The good coach is one who helps his players and team to evaluate the situations which occur on the field. The more correct decisions the players and the team make, the better they will play. The coach makes the complex game, where many diverse situations arise, into a more simple one which the players understand and are confident of playing well.

If a club appoints a coach, it should fall primarily on his shoulders to compile and digest all the apparent strengths and weaknesses not only of his own team but also of each opposition, and to produce an appropriate set of tactics before each game. It is at this stage that the team captain works most closely with the coach, so that between them they finalise a set plan of campaign. It is then up to the captain to ensure that the plan is followed, at least in the opening period of the game.

Assistant coaches

If a club runs one, two or three teams it should be necessary to have only one club coach, but many clubs can boast six or more teams. In this case it is ideal, if appropriate people are available, to have assistant coaches for the various other teams as well as an overall club coach. This is a luxury rather than a necessity, but if such men are available a simple yet effective organisation can be that each coach has two or three teams under his wing to supervise. All club players thus given more personal attention and advice, and each coach can work under one general club policy while varying his work according to his teams' abilities.

Qualifications for a coach

Who then should be these chosen people? It could well be that each team captain has the ability also to coach and organise his players, but good players are not necessarily good captains and good captains are not necessarily good coaches. It has generally been found that a coach should remain completely independent from playing with his team, mainly because he can act as an observer from the sidelines and not have the burden of playing as well and worrying about his own game. It is also generally the case, although not completely so, that you can see far more from the stand or touchline than as a player in one position on the field of play.

Ideally the coach should be an ex-player, having had a good deal of experience on the field of play itself. A person cannot really appreciate the difficulties, situations and pressures that a player faces unless he himself has faced them. You might find a person who has had to give up playing prematurely due to injury but who has kept in touch and studied the game, by attending courses for example.

Keeping up-to-date
Once selected, your club coach should keep himself up-to-date and gain even more knowledge by regularly attending courses given by more experienced and recognised coaches at district, county and national level. Patterns and techniques are ever changing in rugby coaching and it is essential that he is aware of them. The same applies to any assistant coaches.

TRAINING AND PRACTICE

Facilities
Any team of any description needs at least one team training session per week if it has any hope of success. Ideally evenings during the week, starting at say 7 pm, should be set aside for training, depending on a club's facilities. If, for example, a club cannot floodlight a large enough area, alternative arrangements must be made. There could be Sunday morning training, which is adopted by some clubs. It can be very difficult to bear regularly, especially if the players have had an exacting game the day before – not

to mention exacting post-match celebrations. Or it may be possible to use for evening training a local school gymnasium, sports hall, air force hangar or other large indoor area. These are useful substitutes although not as beneficial as outdoor training. Fitness training can be carried out and scrums, lineouts, rucks and mauls practised quite well but team skills, particularly running back play, are just about impossible. Set ploys can be practised and basic techniques coached up to a point, but not as well as in the exact playing conditions afforded by Sunday morning training.

Equipment
The equipment for a training session will consist of as many balls as possible (at least one between four players), canes, flags, posts and traffic cones for grids and channels, tackle bags and a scrummage machine. There should also be access to multi-gym facilities for fitness and weight training.

The grids and channels referred to are ways of dividing the training area. A grid is an area about ten yards square in which a small group of players can practise a skill such as handling. A channel runs right across the area and is used for practising lateral passing, close-support passing and setting up rucks and mauls.

Organisation
Once the training facilities have been organised it is a question of 'when' and 'who'. If a permanent floodlit area is available and a club has, say, six or more teams, different nights have to be set aside for training. Teams should train twice weekly, in which case a suitable plan for a large club might be:

Sunday, 10 am–12.30 pm: mini-rugby and schoolboy rugby. An all-day course should also be held twice during the season for schoolboys (ages 13–19).
Monday, 7–8.30 pm: 5th, 6th and 7th XVs.

Tuesday, 7–8.30 pm: 1st, 2nd, 3rd and 4th XVs.
Wednesday, 7–8.30 pm: 3rd, 4th, 5th, 6th and 7th XVs.
Thursday, 7–8.30 pm: 1st and 2nd XVs.
Friday: no training.

Aims

The aims of a coaching session are:

1. To develop the potential of all individuals in the side by improving their general and positional skills, their fitness, their technique and their tactical appreciation.
2. To improve the units within the side: the ball winning of the forwards and the ball using of the backs. Possession is the key to attack and handling is the key to using the ball effectively once in possession. Also to improve the units' defence and achieve a balanced pressure and cover defence.
3. To develop a style of play, team plan and set ploys in which the fifteen players are involved and enjoy their play.

No session is typical as each must be geared to the particular needs of the individuals, units and teams at that stage of the season. Normally the *first session* of the week will concentrate on:

1. Individual technique.
2. Individual skills.
3. Unit skills.
4. Fitness.

The *second session* will concentrate on:

1. Analysis of the previous week's performance and of next Saturday's opponents.
2. Unit skills.
3. Team practice, with emphasis on the game plan and on the introduction of new strategies or counters.

11

Method

Fitness and skill should not be sought haphazardly. You must have a plan or schedule to give your efforts structure and direction. The major principles are overload, progression, regularity and specificity.

Overload is the basis upon which any programme will stand. It simply means doing more than one is ordinarily used to doing, pushing the mind and the body to extra amounts of work.

Progression is closely related to overload. It is moving towards increasing levels of overload, since overload which remains constant becomes in time underload and stops progression. Progression in technique and fitness can be achieved by increasing the number of repetitions and setting more difficult targets; progression in skill by increasing the speed, the pressure of the opposition, or both.

Regularity is essential. Progression and overload will never have a chance to operate in a programme which is done only once in a while.

Specificity means that fitness and skills must be developed in a programme geared to the needs of the individual.

INDIVIDUAL CLINICS

Technique is the physical mastery of the movements required to perform any given skill; it follows that every player can become to a degree more skilful by becoming more efficient technically. For example, by improving his body position as he takes the ball, a slow passer may find that he can take the ball earlier and thus transfer it quicker.

Each player must recognise that his performance on the field directly affects the success or failure of his team. Some players are aware of their weaknesses and mistakes and work hard to improve them, but most need help and this is where the 'clinic' is useful. Weaknesses in technique, skill or performance in any department can be identified and positive steps taken. Technique can be improved by

12

individual practice; skill can be improved by pressure, either by demanding greater speed in execution or by introducing opposition.

A player may be taught not only to make use of the options available to him in a given situation but also to increase the number of options. Aspects of the game which the player has previously not understood properly may be explained so that he can see and recognise situations in the game as they develop. He must understand fully what is happening if he is to decide on the right course of action. The clinic thus gives the chance to increase a player's technical efficiency by pointing out tactical considerations and suggesting positive solutions.

LEARNING THE BASIC SKILLS

As a player, you should do all in your power to improve your basic skills, particularly those at which you are weak. Practice should be done in addition to and not instead of practice with your team.

Learn a technique until you are confident of the 'feel' of the movements, then gradually introduce it into the game. In training, opposition may be passive at first, but gradually increase the pressure until your skill can be performed effectively in a game.

Kicking
The key factors are the position of the hands, the release and contact. Hold the ball in the way you want to make contact, and make sure you release the ball in this position. Straighten the kicking foot. As usual, work from technique to skill, and by gradually building up opposition pressure develop the screw, grub, chip, garryowen, defensive, attacking and cross kicks.

Running
Develop the sidestep, swerve, change of pace, dummy pass etc. Work particularly hard on the weaker side of your

body: a skilful runner like Gerald Davies causes great concern among defenders because they know he can change direction off either foot and beat them on the inside and the outside with swerve or sidestep. If you can only go one way you are predictable and therefore easy to mark.

Having beaten a defender, accelerate away. Practice continually one against one from all sorts of angles, gradually increasing the amount of space available. As often as possible run with the ball in two hands. Develop the ability to scan the rest of the field while running.

Contact
In attack learn to 'strike' through gaps and to 'break' tackles. Backs use the hips rather than dropping the shoulder; forwards make contact more by dropping the shoulder and barging through.

Handling
Practise receiving from all angles, at different speeds and distances and passing at speed. Taking a pass from the left is usually easier because most people are right-handed, but remember that passing in the same direction, ie. to the right, is more difficult because it involves more use of the left hand.

Close support
Unopposed. With a group of four:

1. One of the four carries the ball. He runs forward and then turns. As he turns he holds the ball out for the next player to take. This player runs and then turns, again holding the ball out for the next man, and so on down the field.
2. One of the four carries the ball. He runs forwards and then turns. Again as he turns he lobs the ball up for the supporting player to take. He in turn passes it on in the same fashion. The group continue down the field, continually turning and passing.

3. The ball carrier runs forwards and falls to the ground. As he falls he turns and either lobs the ball up for the following player or holds it up. In either case the next player drives on until he too falls to the ground and transfers the ball. As soon as a player falls to the ground he must make every effort to get up and join in again.

These drills are useful because they incorporate most of the basics involved in close support play. They are particularly useful to young players but they do lack one essential ingredient – physical contact.

Opposed. With a group of six forwards, four of the group are spaced at ten-metre intervals, one behind the other. The ball carrier and his support player then run towards the first defender. The carrier drives into him and makes the ball available to his support. He in turn drives into the second man in the line and makes the ball available to the supporting player. This goes on until the last man in the line is reached. This drill can be modified to accommodate the various types of ball transfer.

Scrummaging
The ideal is thirty to fifty per week, concentrating on foot positioning, the snap shove, lock mechanics and channelling and delivering the ball. Practise, too, the eight-man shove, wheel and strike against the head on the opposition's ball, and back-row moves.

Lineout
Practise the thow-in, jumping and support for a normal lineout but also variations: three big men together at front, middle or back, two-man, three-man and four-man lines, peels at the front or back, drives in the middle of the line.

COACHING THE UNIT

The performance of the unit is analysed and corrective

measures or new tactics, or both, are introduced to improve its performance. This coaching of the unit might be seen as the therapy part of coaching.

For example, if the forwards' ball winning at the lineout has been poor, it may be improved by corrective measures – improving the co-ordination between the thrower, the jumpers and the supporters – or by changing tactics and introducing the two-man, three-man or four-man line.

TEAM PRACTICE

A team practice should seek to establish a pattern within the game plan: eg. how to receive the ball at the kick-off, how to develop a technique of taking short penalties, when to use particular ploys and how to counterattack when the opposition loses the ball. The practice will vary from week to week, depending on the demands of the next game to be played.

Unopposed

This is very valuable to improve awareness: the whole team can become familiar with all the moves and calls, the backs can recognise the forwards' aims and methods, and the forwards can learn to react properly to the backs' moves. It can also provide practice in all the set pieces and can be used to set up second-phase and third-phase possession.

Opposed

To improve general team skills as opposed to technique, some form of pressure must be placed on the team. Players must be placed in a situation where they must make decisions, and only opposition can really provide this. It does not have to be 15 v 15.

15 v 9. With a pack plus a scrum-half in opposition, scrums, lineouts, rucks and mauls can be set up in almost realistic situations, while the backs can concentrate on moving the ball at speed.

15 v 7. A threequarter line only in opposition allows the pack to concentrate on setting up ruck and maul, while the backs practise using second-phase and third-phase ball effectively.

15 v 3. Any small unit in opposition can put on pressure to improve a particular aspect of play. For example, two half-backs and a back can kick the ball at the team so that they may practise their counterattack.

PHYSICAL FITNESS

The purpose of this book is not to tell you how to get fit; that can be done by your coach or other qualified person. They will aim to build up your stamina, speed and strength, without which you will never play to your full potential of skill for a whole game. Do not play at getting fit but work at it systematically: physical conditioning is like filling a reservoir, and there is no way you can take out what has not been put in, so make sure you keep the reservoir full. An unfit player lets himself down as well as his team-mates.

4

Team Strategy

To enable any team to function at its best it must have a style of play, strategy or team plan which all the players understand and should be capable of putting into operation. This team strategy is generally determined by the strengths and weaknesses of both the individuals and the units in the side. It would be shortsighted for a large club with many teams and a number of squads to have a rigid overall club strategy, but it is possible to promote a uniform policy of play throughout the club, keeping it flexible and adaptable to circumstances.

STRATEGY DICTATED BY TALENT AVAILABLE

Forwards

If a coach sees that he has a particularly large and heavy squad, with sizeable locks and a big back row, he can think of developing a style of play based on kicking for position to obtain scrums and lineouts, followed by moves close to the forwards such as scrum-half breaks, back-row moves, or moves bringing the ball back towards the forwards who should gain second-phase possession and so create scoring opportunities.

If however his available players up front are unusually light and mobile the coach should develop a style of play whereby the ball is directed by swift lateral passing or diagonal kicking away from the opposing pack. The aim is then for his lighter forwards to develop speed over the field in order to get to second-phase situations quicker than the opposition and in greater numbers. He would also introduce such variations as more short lineouts than usual, taking tap penalties rather than kicking to touch, and kicking off away from the forwards to the open spaces to catch the opposition unawares.

Threequarters

The backs' pattern of play depends to a large extent on their forwards, but it should also take account of individual talents and flair. For example, a winger or centre may be very fast and able to beat most opponents by sheer speed, given room to move; in this case he must be fed the ball as early as possible to give him space to manoeuvre. If he is exceptionally strongly built he does not need as much room, but he should still be fed the ball early so that he can gain as much momentum as possible to run at his opposite number and to make a complete break or a half-break.

If a winger or centre's main attribute is a well executed sidestep or jink, which is very difficult to combat, he probably needs less time to manoeuvre, although in any situation a player should be given as much room and time to move as possible.

Scrum-half

To take another example, at scrum-half you may have a player whose pass is short, quick and accurate rather than long and erratic. Although not an exceptionally strong kicker of the ball, perhaps he can run well and break quickly from the scrum. Or your scrum-half may kick well and pass long but be less happy playing a running game. It is the coach's strategic decision, along with the selectors, to decide which qualities prove best for his team's style of play. If there are two scrum-halves in his squad with completely different attributes, one may be preferred for his style of play, but the other may often have to fill his place because of injury or unavailability. In this situation it is conceivable that a coach may change the whole team's style of play, or he may try to encourage the replacement at scrum-half to fit in with the rest of the team.

Fly-half

A fly-half might be an exceptionally good tackler, so his role would be to go up with his centres and tackle and worry his opposing fly-half rather than to act in a sweeping role. (Similarly a centre with the same talent should be encouraged to try to shake the confidence of his opposing centre with some particularly hard tackling.) A less strong-tackling fly-half might be assigned a more sweeping role, covering across and leaving the main task of stopping the opposing fly-half to his back-row forwards. By covering across he can help the centres and wings to deal with any missed tackle or chip over their heads. He also helps the full-back in clearing kicks ahead.

A combination of both sorts of fly-half play might be used: an example is when from scrums and lineouts the fly-half's job is to cover back or across, but from rucked or mauled second-phase ball he closely marks his opposite number. As ever, it is for the coach or captain to decide his pattern of play.

Full-back

A full-back might be particularly big and strong and thus have the ability to hold on to and make available any ball that he has fielded. His team-mates should be made aware that as long as they give him adequate support, they should get possession from the ensuing maul. Again, the full-back might be an exceptionally devastating tackler. In this case his team-mates should be aware of it and retire quickly on the assumption that their player will almost certainly stop his man in a situation where an opponent has only the full-back between himself and the try line.

Individual weaknesses

These are in a sense the reverse of the talent available. Weaknesses in catching, kicking, contact, handling, passing and tactical awareness are all fundamental, and a coach and selectors must decide when selecting their team and planning its strategy the relative strengths and weaknesses of the players available. Coaching and training should concentrate on eradicating such weaknesses.

SELECTION POLICY

A proper selection policy is a very important part of a club's strategy, and a number of options are open. A selection committee of non-players (usually and ideally ex-players) plus the club coach and captain can work well. If a club has numerous teams each respective team coach or captain may be included when selection of that team is made. Using this system the non-players can each observe different teams and a good, overall picture of the players' performances can be made up.

On the other hand a club may well be happy with just the coach and captain, or even the coach on his own, picking the team. Whatever happens, coach and captain should be involved with a team's selection. They work closely together and the captain may be aware of reasons for on-field failures of which even the coach has no immediate knowledge. Selection and coaching go hand in hand to such an extent that the coach must be a member of the selection committee. The style of play is determined by the individuals within the side, and each player should be selected to do a job as part of the coach's overall plan.

Liaison

Players should never be left in the dark as to why they have been demoted to lower teams or for that matter promoted a team. A well organised club ensures that the liaison between selection and the players is beyond reproach.

'No train, no play'

It has been found that the more successful clubs of recent years have been those employing this principle as part of

21

their selection policy. All players, whether it is their first or twenty-first season with the club, should be prepared to comply with the club's training and selection policy. It can be reasonably flexible if, say, a player trains regularly but for some reason which is perfectly acceptable to the other players he cannot train one particular week; to leave him out for that week's game would be harsh.

Instances do occur of a particularly gifted player joining a club but finding himself unable to attend training because of work or travel difficulties. The club then has to decide whether to pick him or not. Is it in the best interests of the club to play him, or would the other players find it unacceptable? Whatever the decision, all the players must be informed.

Horses for courses

Selection policy should be adaptable to specific matches. For example, one fly-half might be a far better kicker than another in the squad, and so more suitable for a match in which the team is expected to be under more severe pressure than usual.

The condition of the pitch can also influence selection. For example, if the ground is likely to be dry and firm the selectors could pick more elusive, trickier and quicker backs; but if the pitch is wet and heavy, not conducive to swift handling and elusive running, they may take advantage of the situation by choosing a kicking fly-half together with bigger and heavier centres. This method of selection should not be introduced too often, since players should be able to adjust to any type of weather and ground conditions, but it has been used and is not without its merits.

Withdrawals

The withdrawal of a player through injury may lead to the late introduction of a player whose position is primarily that of the unavailable player. Alternatively, the selectors may reshuffle; for example, if a 1st XV centre withdraws, the selectors may decide to move a wing into the centre and bring in a 2nd XV wing, rather than promoting a 2nd XV centre.

It has been known for no less than the French national selectors to select a half-back combination and then to drop the scrum-half just before the international because the fly-half originally chosen with him has been withdrawn due to injury. They have then re-selected a completely new half-back combination.

THE CAPTAIN

The most important duty of a captain is his responsibility for the tactics adopted by his side during a game. Let us consider then some of the qualities and attitudes that a person should possess that will help him to be a successful captain. In general he must:

1. Be a natural leader.
2. Believe in success. He should try to infuse this attitude in the other members of his team.
3. Be respected by his team. They will then accept any decisions made by him.
4. Know the game thoroughly. He should keep himself up-to-date with developments in the game.
5. Know all his players – their capabilities and the way that they are likely to react to various situations.
6. Be mentally alive all the time. The captain must be continually thinking and varying his tactics to suit the particular situation.

Off the field his duties are to:

1. Prepare the team with the help of the coach for the next game. Go through the probable tactics with the whole team very thoroughly. Make sure everybody understands them.
2. Make certain the team understands any signals which will be used.

3. Tell the pack leader what is expected of him.
4. Ensure that everybody knows which players will have special responsibilities during the game, eg. who will take the penalty kicks and dropouts, who stands on the ten-yard mark when the opposition take a penalty.
5. Make clear to the team their positions at the set pieces.
6. See that a new member of the side is made to feel at home and just as important to the team as the regular members.
7. Build his tactics around his players. Play to his strength and the opponents' weaknesses.
8. Encourage all players to turn up regularly for training and coaching sessions.
9. Foster team spirit.

On the field he must:

1. Make decisions quickly and clearly so that all players are aware of what is happening. Communication between backs and forwards is vital.
2. Not talk too much. Lead more by example, especially towards the end of a game.
3. Continually offer encouragement to the individual.
4. Keep personal control and demand this of the others in the team.
5. Not allow the referee or any of his decisions to put him or his side off the game.
6. Take all the advantages he can in the first half, that is, if he wins the toss.
7. Turn out in clean kit and insist the rest of the team does the same.

Forwards, in the modern game, play such a vital note that it is essential to have a good pack leader. A good pack leader can turn eight average forwards into a formidable pack. To do this he must:

1. Inspire them to work together in a lively fashion.
2. Lead them by example rather than words.
3. Encourage his forwards all the time.
4. Show most of the qualities necessary for a good captain.

Qualifications

If the coach is primarily responsible for putting across the agreed strategy at training sessions, the captain has to apply it on the field of play. Further, he has to decide whether it is proving beneficial or not. If the results are as expected, he should persevere with the agreed plan, which makes his job far easier. However, if things are not going according to plan, he must decide what new approach might regain his team's hold on the game.

The captain must therefore have a keen tactical sense, but he must also be a natural leader and motivator. Captains come in many different disguises. There is the shouting, aggressive sort. Those who played under Roger Michaelson will recognise this type. He had the ability to bring the best out of his players by this approach, but many others have tried to do the same and have usually failed. Not many have the personality for it, and can succeed only in turning honest players into sullen non-triers. The opposite sort of leader, at least in his early days, was Mervyn Davies. He very seldom shouted but players responded to him and he led principally by example. As he grew older he too became more demonstrative but never came anywhere near the Michaelson class. So, captains beware. Use the approach that best suits your personality, and know how each player responds. A tirade of abuse will stimulate one and destroy another.

Position

The man who best meets the qualifications in the preceding paragraph should be the right captain, regardless of where he plays. But if more than one player is suitable, the question of their positions may be considered. Thus full-back and wing are usually too remote from the action to make their presence felt, while a front-five forward normally has enough to worry about, playing in a hard and strenuous position, without the added responsibility of captaincy. The style of play can also be a factor: fly-half or even centre is a suitable position from which to captain a team dedicated to a flowing style, but if forward-dominated rugby is the plan, those positions would obviously not be as suitable for a captain as would, say, the back row.

Back-row forwards and half-backs tend to develop a natural feeling for tactics as they are responsible for making so many decisions at source. They must be able to assess each situation quickly and to take strong immediate action; players who do this naturally must be good candidates for captaincy. In particular, the scrum-half links with both forwards and backs; he can provide encouragement and impart information easily to all his players, and can also dictate the nature of the play.

In recent years the following players from the 'pivot five' positions were honoured with the captaincy of their countries:

Mervyn Davies, Wales (no. 8)
Tony Neary, England (flanker)
Jacques Fouroux, France (scrum-half)
Andie Leslie, New Zealand (no. 8)
Morne du Plessis, South Africa (no. 8)
John Hipwell, Australia (scrum-half)
Roger Uttley, England (no. 8)
Phil Bennett, Wales and British Lions (fly-half)
Douglas Morgan, Scotland (scrum-half)
Jean-Pierre Bastiat, France (no. 8)
John Moloney, Ireland (scrum-half)
Terry Cobner, Wales (flanker).

5

Match Tactics

BEFORE THE MATCH

Assessing the opposition

When preparing for a particular match, a coach should if possible have a good knowledge of his opposition's abilities, their strengths and their weaknesses. This should not be as difficult as it sounds, because most teams, whether first, second or third class, have basically the same fixture list from season to season, and it is often drawn from clubs within a reasonable radius, so it is not too hard to watch the opposition during their other matches. Besides this scouting, there is past experience, experience of other teams against the opponents, press reports, television or video-tape.

Counters may be organised to the opposition's strengths, individual, unit and team, or tactics and moves planned to take advantage of weaknesses. For example, the team which tries to play a running, handling game from all positions may well find itself in trouble against a team concerned only with smashing down movements. The ball may have to be played behind the opposition, and kicking for position or to drive the other team back may be the best tactic to adopt against this negative approach.

Similarly, the physical condition of the opposition has a bearing on the rhythm and the speed of your own team's game. The fitter an opponent, the greater the control and variety of play needed to overcome him. If you are technically superior, the object of your fit opponent must be to pressure you and to make you hurry your game. Patience

27

and strong nerves are needed to keep you in the game until your opponent tires and can be beaten. It is as well to remember that your opponent is human, with a certain degree of fitness, and with strengths and weaknesses in his character. In a contact game such as rugby some players are nervous and may lose confidence during the game if they are attacked hard or make a few mistakes early on. A clever player will take advantage of this weakness in an opponent and play on it.

Attacking the opposition's weaknesses

In attack, your tactics will concentrate on the opposition's weaknesses, as long as in doing so you do not reveal your own weaknesses. For example, a tackling weakness in any of the opposition's threequarter line should be immediately exploited by the weak tackler's actual opponent or by his immediate opponent at any moment during play. An initial breakthrough can be made if he is the first line of defence and perhaps a scoring breakthrough if he is the last line of defence. Similarly, a lack of genuine speed and mobility around the field in an opposing full-back can be exploited by kicking away from him or over his head, and attempting either to regain possession before he arrives at the ball to clear the situation or even to catch him in possession. It may also be worth trying to run round him if you are carrying the ball, particularly if you are a winger who has been given the ball with enough room to move.

Using the opposition's strengths

Sometimes the strength of an opposing team's style of play can be turned to your own advantage. A good example is a team who are renowned for open, fluid rugby involving quick movement of the ball along the threequarters. This style of play can be attacked, as long as you know it beforehand, much more easily than a pattern of play which is dominated by forwards. In defence your threequarters should be exceptionally quick up in to the tackle, particularly in the centre, hoping to catch the man in possession or to worry him into giving a wild pass. In attack, kicking ahead may find open areas left by a full-back who is particularly keen on joining his threequarter line, while organised following of kicks ahead by as many players as possible should draw mistakes from the counterattack that may be predicted as part of this team's style of play.

The individual ability of the opposition must also be considered. If, for instance, an opposing scrum-half or fly-half is a renowned kicker of the ball, your full-back and wings should be more prepared to hang back to regain possession from attacking kicks. As coach, you must also take into consideration such factors as the keenness of an opposition full-back to attack, or the use of his power by an opposing centre or wing. Your own threequarters should be made aware of such factors before the game.

Recent performances
A coach must analyse effectively the performance of his team as individuals, units and a team, and if necessary must take positive measures to adapt the overall strategy to produce the best results.

ON THE FIELD

Pitch and weather conditions
Match tactics start to be formed before the match begins, when the coach and players inspect the pitch and the weather prospects an hour before the game.

The size of the pitch. This will have a great bearing on how a team can play. A narrow pitch limits threequarter play, while a wide pitch may give faster players more opportunity to run. The size of the in-goal area is also a very important consideration, as a large in-goal area is more difficult to defend and diagonal kicks to fast wingers may lead to tries.

Slope. Any slope on the pitch may often be used to advantage by kicking half-backs.

The condition of the pitch. Whether it is firm, wet,

muddy or bone hard will affect the type of stud to be worn and often the method of attack.

The sun. This can be a very disturbing factor in one of the two halves, making the fielding of high kicks very difficult for the full-back and wings. It may disappear behind trees, houses, the stand or clouds. This possibility will have a bearing on the choice of ends.

The wind. Playing with the wind, the half-backs and full-back should use it to gain long touches. Kick high so that the wind can carry the ball. Even if touch is missed, ground is likely to be gained and it is unlikely that the return kick will gain much ground. The team playing against a strong wind can be completely frustrated by being driven back by these long, hoisted kicks. When playing with the wind, the full-back may not position himself as deep as usual. All players must be aware that the ball is likely to hang in the air when the opposition kicks the ball to them and they must be prepared to move forward onto it. If the three-quarters are likely to launch a handling attack the passing must be particularly accurate and players must be aware that the wind may carry the ball away from them. Wingers must be prepared to chase the long kicks in order to take advantage of defensive mistakes and also to stifle any counterattack.

Playing against the wind, half-backs and full-back should kick low and aim for a safe touch rather than distance; the low torpedo kick will make most ground against the wind. The full-back and wings must position themselves deeper as the opposition will kick both longer and more often than normal. The plan should be to run the ball back at the opponents and to keep the ball tight when in possession. The team that passes against the wind may often have an advantage as the ball should be coming into them and may be easier to catch. The threequarters may need to have a steeper alignment.

Wet weather. As the ball is likely to be wet and slippery or heavy and muddy, backs will need to stand closer together and each team member must be prepared to kill the loose ball by falling immediately whenever he or one of his team-mates makes a mistake. The lineouts are liable to be very scrappy and sweepers should be used to deliver controlled ball to the scrum-half. The forwards, particularly the loose forwards, should attempt to drive through onto any mistakes. In these conditions the man in possession of the ball has a definite advantage over his opponent as almost every opponent can be eluded, if the ball carrier has enough space, by a feint or a change in direction. The defender is often unable to recover because of the slippery ground. Threequarters must be aware of this potential advantage and make use of it when the situation arises. Half-backs may use high kicks, both the garryowen and into the box, to take advantage of the greasy ball.

Changing the plan

The earlier part of this chapter emphasised the importance of a match plan, and once on the field the team's first intention must be to carry out that plan. Because it should consist of many channels of approach, all of which have been made clear to all the players at the final pre-match briefing, good time must be given for it to prove effective – say twenty to twenty-five minutes in an eighty-minute game. If by then the plan is proving effective there should be no reason to change the style of play. About the only exception is when your side is winning so easily well before the end of a game that it is worth experimenting with other styles of play to see how well the team adapts to them.

However, if the plan is proving unsuccessful and your side has not established dominance, or is even losing, the captain, possibly in consultation with his vice-captain, takes over as 'on-field coach'. He must decide how to vary the tactics to take the initiative from the opposition. For example, if the pre-match plan was to dominate by forward power and kicking for possession, but in the match itself you find that your opposition is gaining at least equal possession or perhaps that your threequarters are clearly superior to those of the opposition, in either case you

31

should adopt a more running, handling, outflanking approach.

To take the opposite case, if you have gained very little by moving the ball away from the forwards and along the threequarter line in order to tire the opposition and to gain good second-phase possession, you should think of other channels of attack. Having considered whether the natural talent in your threequarter line has been fully exploited, you should be thinking in terms of moves which switch the ball back towards your forwards or even of ploys down the middle of the field. Your play should still be based on the fact that your lighter and quicker forwards will get to the breakdown or second-phase first, either carrying the ball on themselves or setting up good second-phase ball through the superiority of numbers at the breakdown. From this second-phase either the ball can be quickly spun across the field, or the scrum-half or a forward can peel around the maul or ruck, closely followed by the rest of the pack once again, with the intention of setting up good third-phase ball.

If kicking high and ahead has so far not had much place in your tactics, this should certainly be tried by either the scrum-half or the fly-half. Or the wingers may try high crosses infield. Even short chips ahead by the fly-half or centres, just over the opposing threequarters' heads, could change the course of the game.

If you have exposed any weaknesses in the opposing defence, your amended plan should of course aim to work on these.

If the change of tactics proves successful it should be carried on, but if you still find yourself up against it, look for the assistance of individual talent. For example, if both the scrum-half and the fly-half have been acting merely as a link, each could now be encouraged to run with the ball in an attempt to make definite breaks past the opposition. Or, if one of your centres is of a powerful physique but has so far been playing a quick-passing game, it would be time for him to use his power and attempt to burst through the opposition either immediately or following a set move such as a scissors. A winger might have quite exceptional pace but be in a team whose pattern of play has been an attempt to dominate with the forwards. He should now be given more of the ball, with room to move, and given a chance to outpace his opposition either by carrying the ball or by kicking ahead and chasing. Encourage the full-back, if he has not come into the line very often, at least to try to create an extra man. In extreme situations, a centre and a winger, or the two wings, might change positions so that, for example, your strongest tackler is marking a particularly dangerous runner on the other side.

The score line will obviously have an important bearing on the tactical plan. When sitting on a narrow lead at the end of a close game, it is important to realise how to keep the lead by kicking for touch and by avoiding making mistakes as the time ticks away. A team which is losing narrowly may be expected to take more chances, for example attacking from its own line or taking short penalties instead of kicking for goal if the deficit is more than four points.

Communication

Communication between team-mates can play a very important role. Players should be prepared to talk to each other quickly in any situation. Whether the other man on your side knows what you are going to do can make the vital difference.

TACTICAL REMINDERS

1. Test your opponent to discover his strengths and weaknesses.
2. Vary your attack to keep your opponent guessing about the type of attack being used.
3. Aim to establish the tempo of the game according to your own strengths.
4. Play on your opponents' weaknesses.

33

5. Force your opponent to play to your strengths.
6. Always play to a plan rather than with reckless abandon; maintain your plan of attack if you are successful; revise your tactics if you are losing.
7. Anticipate your opponents' reaction and plan additional strategies as you play.
8. Concentrate on the game situation rather than the score.

6

The Individual Player

ATTITUDE

Confidence in your own ability, no matter who the opposition is, should be instilled in you by your coach and captain before you take the field. You should always approach a match with a positive attitude and with the primary intention of attacking the opposition with the forces and talents at your disposal, rather than adopting a defensive attitude right from the start.

Concentration is the ability to perform in a game what has been practised in training. Relaxation, in this context, is the opposite to concentration. Most players know the basics and, when asked, can give the correct answers to questions about their function, but not to do what has been thoroughly rehearsed is a rugby sin. It does not matter how many times a technique has been practised in training, if it is not done correctly on the field all that training has been a waste of time. For example, if a lineout peel is called but instead the ball is mistakenly thrown to the front, the whole side suffers because of the thrower's lack of concentration.

Determination is the desire to resist and finally to overcome, and must be part of the make-up of every rugby player. Domination does not come easily but is the result of hard work. Every player must not only want to dictate to his opposite number, he must want to overwhelm him, to demolish the opposition.

Pressure causes errors in play and faulty judgement. A player must not only learn to exert pressure but, often

more importantly, he must have the mental strength to remain calm and controlled when under pressure himself.

INDIVIDUAL TACTICAL APPRECIATION

Not only should individuals have the ability to carry out the coach's game plan; each player will often have to vary his own play according to situations over which the captain himself probably has no direct control, less still the coach. It is then that a player's tactical appreciation or lack of it is discovered.

A fly-half, for instance, may not notice that an opposing full-back has been very weak at picking up a rolling ball (it is easier to spot the more obvious weakness of dropping a high ball) and thus persists in kicking high when grubber kicks or chips ahead would be far more effective. Or a centre, with the opposing winger between him and the try line, might choose to kick over his head and chase, not having the tactical appreciation to realise that this particular winger has missed at least two easy tackles earlier in the game.

Another example would be a full-back, confronted with two opposing players for the first time. Being the last line of defence, he may have the sense to remember that the player with the ball in his hands has, in the majority of

1 *(opposite, above)*. Gerald Davies, in a tight situation near the corner flag during the Wales v. Ireland match of 1975, shows his commitment and determination in a low, aggressive dive. This makes a conventional tackle or a body-check by a defender that much harder, and in this case Wally McMaster cannot prevent the score.

2 *(opposite, below)*. J. P. R. Williams' famous body-check on Jean-François Gourdon in the dying minutes of Wales v. France at Cardiff, 1976. The flag in the picture is the corner flag and had Gourdon scored, Wales would almost certainly have lost the match and their seventh Grand Slam. JPR's determination and complete commitment are evident, although Gourdon made himself an easier target by keeping his body upright. Is the photographer in the background looking so glum because he has just missed an historic photo or because he is a Frenchman?

cases during the game up to now, attempted a dummy on reaching an opponent. This being the case, a player with good tactical appreciation would expect yet another dummy and would concentrate more on full-blooded tackling of the ball carrier than on delaying a would-be tackle slightly in order to force a pass or to gain an interception.

INDIVIDUAL FLAIR

Drills develop technique but they do not develop judgement, the gift of doing the right thing at the right time. A player can be presented with a series of alternatives by his coach, but which to use in a given situation remains his decision. If a forward, he alone can judge whether to drive on or to turn. If a back, he can follow few set rules about performing a counterattack but must improvise. The good player is the one who makes the right decision most of the time.

It is also up to the individual not only to appreciate what tactics should be used but also to revert in a moment to another tactic if necessary. An example of this would be when an acceptable set ploy has been called, say a miss pass from the inside centre straight to the full-back entering the line. But the fly-half, on going to pass the ball, sees in that split second that the move has no chance of success because the opposition is coming up so fast on his threequarters. His natural flair tells him that a kick diagonally over the opposing threequarters' heads should give his open-side winger a much better chance of a try. Such an ability to take split-second decisions is given to very few rugby players at any level of the game, but it can be developed.

Flair has a lot to do with confidence, the confidence in your own ability with which this chapter began. You will find at any level of rugby that the players who appear to possess that extra something are the ones who have confidence in their own ability at that level, coupled with discipline. The words 'at that level' are important, as a junior club player or even a schoolboy can show it at his particular standard. At international level, one can sense the complete self-confidence in their own ability of players like Mike Gibson of Ireland or J. P. R. Williams of Wales, unlike many others on the international field with them. It is largely an inborn quality but often it can be taught by patience, understanding, encouragement and guidance.

7

The Forwards

THE FRONT FIVE

Role

The role of the front five is that of primary ball getters. The best backs in the world cannot play without the ball, while the flankers and no. 8 feed off the success of the front five; if the opposition is always going backwards the back row shines. Games at the highest levels are won and lost by the front five, for although a side can still win if it gets only forty per cent of the ball, with only twenty per cent its chances of success are almost nil.

Special characteristics

To succeed as a front-five forward demands a special type of person. It is not enough to be big, although it helps. It is not enough to be strong, although it helps. It is not enough to be fit, although it is essential. Above all, front-five forwards must have determination and aggression; without these attributes they are nothing. The whole pack must work as a unit but the front five must work as a unit within that unit, work until they are ready to drop. A good front-five forward never surrenders.

All players must possess the basic skills of passing, catching, kicking and tackling. In addition, forwards must develop unit skills to a very high degree. Scrummaging must become second nature to forwards, although it is not an essential for backs. (J. P. R. Williams would probably disagree – because of injuries he played as an emergency flanker in one test in Australia in 1978.) Despite this extra burden on forwards they must not neglect or ignore the fundamental individual skills. Forwards do not get many opportunities to kick but when they have to they should be able to do so without the backs falling over with laughter.

In addition to the skills necessary for backs, forwards have to develop many individual skills of their own. These skills are usually necessary because of the close contact in which forwards normally find themselves; they normally depend on the presence of other supporting forwards but are nevertheless individual skills. Their aim is to maintain continuity, a favourite word of Ray Williams, WRU Coaching Organiser. Individual skills are best learnt young, like riding a bicycle – once learnt they are never completely forgotten. But the level must be maintained by constant practice until these skills become part of the player.

Not only must a front-five forward of today do his job in the set pieces, he must also contribute to the loose play. Gone are the days when a prop trudged from scrum to scrum and a lock ambled from lineout to lineout. The game has become much more arduous for the front five as greater responsibilities have been thrust upon them.

Finally, although each forward must want to dominate, the function of the forwards must be to operate as a unit. 'One for all and all for one' is an apt motto for any pack.

THE BACK ROW

Role
The role of the flankers and the no. 8 is made up of several different functions. The loose forwards are:

1. Ball winners. They contribute actively to lineout, scrum, maul and ruck.
2. Link players. They provide the support and continuity to the attack by being in good support positions, by handling quickly and by winning the ball from ruck and maul.

3. Distributors. Like the half-backs, part of the job is distribution, particularly from the scrum (no. 8) and the tight-loose.
4. Ball users. They initiate their own attacks, using their handling skill.
5. Pressure players. They provide bone-crushing tackles in a pressing defence, or last ditch tackles in defensive cover.
6. Tactical pivots. They are, with the half-backs, the players best suited to implement or change the agreed pattern of play or tactics. By their position between the front five and the back five, they are most able to dominate tactics and to influence play accordingly.

Special characteristics
Alertness. The loose forward must react immediately to shifts from attack to defence. Lightning reactions will put him in the right place at the right time, either to take advantage of any openings in attack or to cover unguarded opponents in defence. Ability does not mean anything without a level of alertness. The loose forward must be able to size up him immediate opponents quickly and then to capitalise upon this knowledge. He must constantly assess the opponents' abilities, noticing their speed, cleverness, general strengths and weaknesses and methods of attack and defence.

Determination. This is essential in every phase of the game. It can be described as self-confidence, the will to win and the desire to outplay every opponent. It is wanting to beat one's opponent all the time and going after him time and again in order to dominate him in attack and to pressure him in defence.

Reading the game. The quality which separates the top loose forwards from the ordinary ones. Reading the game is the ability to understand what is happening, to anticipate immediate and future developments and to exploit the knowledge boldly and intelligently. Good players have a natural capacity for it, while others must develop it.

Stamina-hustle. One of the most important qualities of the loose forward. However skilful or quick the player may be, he will be of little value to his team during a hard match unless he has the endurance to do these capabilities justice. The loose forward must be able to cover a lot of ground purposefully, never aimlessly, and he must have the mobility to set up intelligent positions in his continual search for the ball. His constant movement and alertness enable him to capitalise on any errors by his opponents.

Speed. Loose forwards must be able to think fast, run fast and recover fast. They should aim to be first to the ball, first to support, first to tackle, first to cover.

Strength. No rugby player can become too strong, and strength is essential for the ball winner. The loose forward needs pure 'static' strength, especially in the upper arm and shoulder, to jump, maul, ruck and scrummage. He also needs power/endurance strength to resist fatigue.

Size. The loose forward should be able to dominate his opponent by physical superiority in body weight and bulk in the set pieces and in the tight-loose. He must also contribute to ball winning at the lineout by his greater height, allied to jumping ability and timing. The good big one will beat the good little one providing he can do all the good things the little one can do.

Mobility and agility. The loose forward must have the mobility and agility to adjust to any situation as rapidly as possible. This mobility and agility will enable him to win the ball in the air (lineout), from the floor (loose ball) or from the hand (maul). It will also enable him to adjust quickly when tackling.

Ball using. Ideally the back-row forward should be able to run and handle like a back. He must therefore have all the skills and judgement of the ball user as well as those of the ball winner.

Left and right or open and blind?

Many a debate has raged over the years about the role of

the loose forwards in the game and the system which the loose forwards unit should adopt in the team plan. The overseas system – right and left flank – and the British method – open side and blind side – both have their respective advantages and disadvantages. The overseas method shared the load between the two flankers whilst the British method was claimed to be the best way of stopping the opposing fly-half from running, by putting a specialist open-side wing forward to mark him.

In 1968 Ray Williams and the Welsh Coaching Advisory Committee produced a paper on back-row play which revolutionised loose-forward play in Wales and in Britain. The paper established the fact that the loose forward was primarily a ball winner and not simply a defence against the opposing half-backs, and therefore advocated the acceptance of the right and left flanker system instead of the open side and blind side system. Ray Williams justified this revolution by pointing to developments in the last decade which led him to believe that the right and left flanker system would be the more effective:

1. Ruck and maul ball can be more valuable than the ball from the set piece. The loose forwards are committed to winning the ball, so they must arrive first at the breakdown to continue or originate the attack.
2. The change in laws at scrum, ruck and maul has limited the forward movement of the loose forwards until the ball has emerged.
3. Loose forwards now initiate attacks from the lineout, scrum, ruck and maul and similarly need to defend against such attacks.
4. Eight forwards are needed to participate actively in winning the ball at ruck and maul.

Under the style of play suggested by Ray Williams, a flanker can concentrate much of his energy on winning the ball for his side, while the fly-half accepts the responsibility for looking after his own man. Similarly, in recent years deep cover for the team has been provided by the blind-side wing, which has meant that the no. 8 has played a role more like that of the flank forward. He is able to concentrate on getting nearer to the ball and can therefore be more effective as a supporter.

The British Lions sides against the All Blacks in 1971 (the last two Tests) and against South Africa in 1974 reverted to the old British system of an open-side and a blind-side flanker. Responsibility for the open side of the field was that of a fast flank forward like John Taylor or Fergus Slattery, while the blind-side role was given to a new big man. Derek Quinnell, Peter Dixon and Roger Uttley, at near 6 foot 4 inches and 16 stones, are examples of this new animal. Their role was primarily that of the ball winner at the set pieces, while their size and strength and technique were extremely advantageous at the ruck and maul.

Styles of play

The loose forward's style of play depends largely on his own physique, skill and tactical maturity. Only a few players have everything, and some manage very well on just one outstanding talent. The screening for such natural talents must be intelligent, as the player's natural endowments will decide the type of loose forward he should concentrate on becoming.

The blockbuster. This type of player could often be found playing as a lock forward, since he is around 6 foot 4 inches and 16 stones. What distinguishes him from the lock forward is his speed, mobility and ball playing ability. Because of his size and strength he is a great rucker and mauler, and he uses his height to good advantage in the lineout. The Springbok and All Black teams invariably throw up outstanding blockbusters as loose forwards. In recent years Jan Ellis (South Africa), Kel Tremain (New Zealand) and Ian Kirkpatrick (New Zealand) have been leading examples. They have been not only outstanding ball winners with their size and strength, but because of their skill, speed and mobility they have also been a threat

45

in the loose. Each of these players was capable of initiating attacks and their superb charging runs have been a feature of their play. Their size and speed made them very difficult to stop. In recent years the British Isles sides have picked players of a similar type as loose forwards: Peter Dixon, Derek Quinnell and Roger Uttley have already been quoted as examples.

The opportunist. This type of loose forward lives off the mistakes of others. He always seems to be there when the fly-half fumbles or the scrum-half makes a bad pass. The old open-side wing forward was an expert at this opportunist game of being in the right place at the right time. The 'easy' try always seemed to go to him but only because he was naturally near the ball. Haydn Morgan (Wales) and Dave Morris (Wales) are good examples of opportunists.

The action man. There are many different physical types who may fit this category. Generally smaller than block-busters, about 6 foot and 14 stones, they are distinguished by their pure speed, stamina, fitness and all-round foot-balling ability. They appear to be in perpetual motion and seem always to be first to the ball. At international level great examples have been Terry Cobner and Trevor Evans (Wales), Tony Neary and Budge Rogers (England), Roger Arneil and Nairn McEwan (Scotland), Fergus Slattery and Noel Murphy (Ireland), and Waka Nathan (New Zealand). All of these caused havoc by their out-standing tackling skills allied to startling speed.

The ball player. Every loose forward must be a ball player, but over the years certain outstanding ball players have distinguished themselves on the international scene. They have come in different sizes and in different positions, representing different countries, but they have all been very creative players, distinguished from others by their reading of the game, their ball handling and their running skills. Examples are: at no. 8, Stuart, Lochore, Leslie (New Zealand), Muller, Hopwood, Bedford, du Plessis (South Africa), Pask, Davies (Wales), Goodall (Ireland), Spanghero and Dauga (France); and at flanker,

Greyling (South Africa), Morgan, Taylor (Wales), Moncla, Crauste, Skrela and Rives (France).

The back row as a unit
The style of play the team adopts will have an important bearing on the type of player selected for the loose-forward unit. The All Blacks and the Springboks have regularly produced large, dominating packs of forwards, and the selection of the loose forwards has helped these packs to crush their opponents by the use of hard, driving forward play. The players selected have generally been two big men, 6 foot 3 inches and over 15 stones, and one smaller man, nearer 6 foot and 14 stones. This combination produces two players with the extra strength, power and drive which will allow them to dominate the set pieces and to set up ruck and maul effectively, and one smaller player capable of providing the extra mobility and ball skill. Tremain, Lochore and Nathan (New Zealand), Ellis, Greyling and Bedford (South Africa), and Davies, Uttley and Slattery (British Lions) were fine examples of this combination.

The Welsh and the French, apparently adopting the right and left flanker system, have produced players of different style and technique. Both sides have three-quarter lines capable of sustaining a fast, running, handling, overlapping, outflanking attack. The ball has moved faster than the man and speed and quick handling ability has been the priority. The composition of the loose forward unit has tended towards two smaller men at flank, with one large player at no. 8. The smaller men support and in many cases create the fast handling attack by their handling and running skills, and the large man dominates the lineout by his height and distributes the ball quickly from the base of the scrum. Taylor, Morris and Davies (Wales) and Rives, Skrela and Bastiat (France) are fine examples. At club level the London Welsh combination of John Taylor and Tony Gray as the smaller mobile pair and Mervyn Davies as the large no. 8 was the best attacking

47

unit to emerge in Britain in recent years. They were magnificent exponents of the running, handling attack.

COUNTERS TO OPPOSITIONS' STRENGTHS

Against a pack dominating the scrum:

1. Lock the scrummage.
2. Put the ball into the scrum as soon as it is formed.
3. Use the nearest channel as it will be the quickest ball.
4. Pack 3-3-2, having two no. 8s to take the pressure off the scrum-half.
5. Pack Andie Leslie fashion, 3-4-1, with the no. 8 between the left flanker and the left lock.
6. Use three-man scrums.
7. Opt for lineouts instead of scrums whenever possible.
8. Eliminate your own mistakes.

Against a pack spoiling the half-backs at the scrum:

1. Produce better quality ball.
2. Hold the ball in the scrum and drive forward.
3. Use back-row moves, particularly the no. 8 picking up.

Against a pack coming through the lineout:

1. Improve the blocking and support.
2. Hold the ball and drive it.

Against a pack dominating the lineout:

1. Use line variations: quick throw, two-man, three-man and four-man lines.
2. Throw the ball over the end of the lineout to the centres, fly-half, scrum-half or nominated forward.
3. Do not kick for touch.

4. Choose scrums wherever possible.

Against a spoiling pack in the tight-loose (ie. close-contact play, as in the immediate area of a breaking scrum or lineout):

1. Tie them in.
2. Drive at your opponents, taking them out before releasing the ball to the threequarters.
3. Use lineout peels at front and back.
4. Use back-row moves from the scrum.
5. Drive from the mauls and rucks to take the fringe players out.

8

The Set Scrum

The success of the Lions in New Zealand in 1971 re-awakened interest in scrummaging all over the world. During that tour, despite losing through injury both first choice props, Ray McLoughlin and Sandy Carmichael, the Lions devastated the New Zealanders. This makes that scrummaging performance even more praiseworthy. More importantly, it shows that scrummaging can be improved enormously with practice; on that tour scrummaging played a big part in almost every training session. Its importance to the overall plan was shown by the fact that even some of the backs took part in scrummaging practice when injury made this necessary. The tour also emphasised the importance of scrummaging technique, and Ian MacLauchlan's ignominious hoisting of Jazz Muller (all eighteen and a half stones of him) out of several scrums indicated what could be done by an extremely able technician to a very big man. The drive which the Lions exerted also limited the chances of New Zealand's scrum-half, Sid Going, and on occasions made him look an ordinary player.

The psychological impact of good scrummaging cannot be over-emphasised. It is an enormous boost to confidence if the opposition's pack is in retreat at every scrum. Furthermore, the tactical advantages of good scrum-maging are immense. It means the opposition have to try to attack from, at best, a standing start.

BINDING

This is the first essential of any tight scrum, and if everyone is bound tightly together before the scrum goes down it makes for greater efficiency. It is very difficult, if not impossible, to convert a loosely bound scrum into a tightly knit formation after the two packs have joined together. So the first essential is to bind tightly before going down.

The aim of tight binding is to make the scrum into one strong unit. If the binding is haphazard and slack, then regardless of the power and technique of the individuals the scrum will not be effective as a unit.

Front row

A loose front row is an easy target for any opposition worth its salt. The hooker normally has his arms over the inside arms and shoulders of his props, under their outside armpits. Hookers in the past have not been too careful about their binding but with a tightening up of the law they are now more circumspect. There are a number of ways in which this binding can be made tighter. Before going down the hooker can bind himself first to the loose head and then, having established a solid grip, can now get as close as possible to the loose head before swinging his right arm round the tight head and bringing the tight head close into him. The hooker and the props are thus very tightly bound before the props actually bind onto the hooker. The props now do this with their inside arms. The point of binding varies but normally the fist is firmly clenched round the lower part of the jersey.

This binding means that not only are the upper parts of the bodies close together but so are the lower parts. The hips of the front row should, in fact, be so close together that it is impossible for the locks to get their heads into position without going very low. This is an added bonus of tight front-row binding.

There are several variations of front-row binding which seem to work for different packs. The one mentioned is probably the most effective and most widely used, but whichever technique is adopted one factor remains paramount – *bind tight*.

A prop's outside arm should bind onto the opposition prop in a legal fashion. This means that the outside arm of the loose-head prop should be inside the outside arm of the opposing tight-head prop. This obviously limits the variations possible but most props through experience find the position that suits them best and their opponent least.

Locks

A lock obviously has two types of binding to think about. The inside arm must be bound around his partner while the outside arm must bind onto the prop in front.

The inside-arm binding should be done first. A useful technique is, having placed the inside arm around the other lock, to grip firmly onto the top of his shorts. This is best done by placing the thumb inside the top of his shorts and then making a fist around the waistband.

The outside arms of the locks pose quite a problem. The most efficient method of binding is to bind between the legs of the prop. The grip should be on the waistband of the prop's shorts. This type of binding may not look very elegant, and sometimes provokes from spectators ribaldly sympathetic remarks aimed at the prop, but it does have several advantages over the older style where the lock bound around the prop's outside leg. The inside-leg method is stronger and allows the lock to use his outside arm more efficiently in pulling the prop in towards the hooker to help achieve a tightly-bound unit.

3 *(opposite, above)*. The result of solid scrummaging by London Welsh against Harlequins, 1977. The pressure on the Harlequins' tight-head prop forces him into an extremely ineffective (and uncomfortable) position.

4 *(opposite, below)*. The Pontypool front row in action for the Lions in New Zealand, 1977. Note that the props and the locks are already bound before the scrum forms. Notice, too, the commitment of the flanker, Jeff Squire, to the scrum.

No. 8

He plays his part in the binding operation by pulling the locks closer together. Although there is theoretically nothing wrong with the no. 8 binding around the inside legs of the locks this position is not normally used. The most common binding is around the locks' hips. Many no. 8s merely go through the motions of tight binding, but to play his full part he must make a definite attempt to pull the locks together.

Flankers

The main initial role of a flanker is to push. Not too long ago this would have been thought absurd but now it is generally accepted that if the scrum is to be effective all eight forwards must pull, or rather push, their weight. A flanker should bind with his inside arm over the nearest lock. This again should not be merely for show and the flanker must make a big effort to bind tightly. The outside hand and arm are normally used to help the drive of the scrum by resting them on the ground and then pushing off them.

All this binding must be done before the scrum goes down to meet the opposition. Once this tightly-knit formation is established it is not easily broken and the scrum is on the way to success.

FOOT POSITIONS

The aim of the pack should be to push the opposition backwards down the field along a line running parallel with the touchline. Both locks push mainly on their props, which tends to push the props outwards. The danger of the loosening or even disintegration of the front row is counteracted most efficiently by the flankers pushing in at an angle on the props. The net result of the two forces operating on the prop is to transmit the shove in a forward direction.

Front row

The positions adopted by the individual members of the front row are different and a number of factors dictate them; for example the hooker's stance will depend on whose put-in it is.

In general, the loose-head prop should adopt a comparatively wide stance, with his left foot further forward than his right foot. This means not only that he can still bind closely to his hooker but also that the ball can emerge comparatively easily, if required, between his legs. A narrow base would also be weaker and make it easier for the opposition tight head to disrupt him. The extent to which the left foot should be forward depends on the individual and the circumstances. If the hooker is under pressure then it might be wise to make the gap wider so that the ball can come back more easily but this in turn leads to a decrease in pushing power. At international level both feet are normally placed quite well back, but again with the left slightly in front of the right.

The tight-head prop will also use different techniques depending on the circumstances, but he normally has his right foot in front of the left, with both feet further back than those of the loose head.

Hookers are lords unto themselves in most packs. However, in the more disciplined and effective packs the hooker's foot position depends on whether he is going to strike for the ball. On his own put-in both feet are initially together and quite far forward but not so far forward that he cannot strike for the ball when it comes in. If his role is to be a pusher, as in an eight-man scrum, then both feet will be considerably further back.

Locks

The feet positions of the locks are a difficult problem. There are many variations but the most efficient and most comfortable for pushing is to have both feet well back but with the outside foot slightly in front of the inside. This gives a good base from which to drive forward. If, however, a locking position is to be taken, then both feet must go right back so that the legs are straight. They must also be spread wide apart and turned outwards; this gives a very strong defensive position.

No. 8

The no. 8's feet naturally have to be well back, otherwise he will get tangled up with the feet of the locks. How far back they are depends on whether it is to be a pushing scrum or a locking scrum, as it does with the locks.

Flankers

The foot position of a flanker is dictated by the direction in which he is going to push on his prop. The greater the angle between the flanker and the prop the further forward will be his feet. As the angle gets smaller so his feet go further back. Again, the outside foot is normally ahead of the inside, and indeed it would be extremely difficult to do it in any other way.

BODY POSITIONS

Every member of the scrum must keep his body position low. All the other things might be being done correctly, but if the scrummage is high then it is not normally very effective. This low position is initially decided by the front row, and how low they go depends on their own ability. Some front rows go so low that the only way the hooker can heel the ball is with his head – which is not to be highly recommended and now is actually illegal. The locks in turn must pack so that they come up and push under the buttocks of the front row. In fact, the locks normally push largely on the props, particularly on their own put-in, to give the hooker a little more freedom. The no. 8 and flankers must aim to push in the same way as the locks – just under the buttocks of the men in front. A general principle to be remembered: a low, tight scrum is a good scrum.

LEG POSITIONS

The positions of the legs of the various forwards depends again on the type of scrum. If the idea is to rush the opposition backwards then the legs will have to be flexed immediately before the ball is put in. As the ball comes in the legs are straightened with a snap and this produces a number of effects. Provided the back and head positions of the forwards are right the immediate response is for the scrum to move forward, if only slightly. Immediately after this initial snap, the pressure is maintained by the rear foot of every man in the scrum moving forward past the leading foot. This continues the drive. It helps considerably if the scrum is so well together that the feet of the individuals all move at the same time. The Newport pack is an extremely good example of this method.

BACK AND HEAD POSITIONS

The other major factor in developing a good scrummage is the position of the forwards' backs and heads. To produce and transmit a good shove the backs of all the members of the scrum should be straight at the moment of push. This in turn is helped if the heads of the forwards are up. If the effort is made to lift the head then it almost automatically follows that the back will be straight. Conversely, once the head goes down this usually means that the efficiency of the push has gone down with it.

CHANNELLING

Winning the ball on your own put-in is not enough. The ball must be controlled and it must emerge from the scrum at the best place.

Position A (see page 58) is the ideal place as it gives the scrum-half maximum protection. The hooker must sweep the ball back with his right foot (not just stick out a foot and hope that the ball emerges somewhere on his side) so

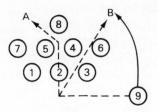

Channelling the ball at the set scrum

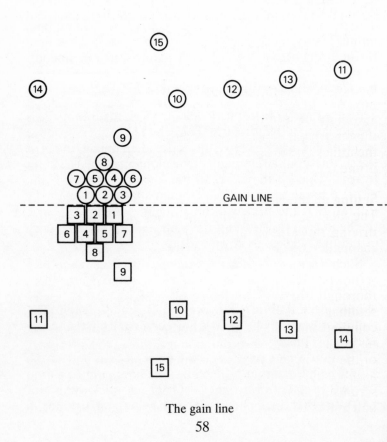

The gain line

58

that it travels between the locks to the no. 8, who uses his feet to set the ball up for the scrum-half.

Position B is sometimes useful if the scrum is under extreme pressure: although he has less protection, the scrum-half may be able to clear the ball before his pack is pushed back. It is also convenient for launching some back-row moves (see pages 62–3). The hooker knocks the ball back to emerge between the left-hand lock and flanker.

ATTACK FROM THE SET SCRUM

The gain line
The primary object of any attack is to cross the gain line, an imaginary, ever-changing line running across the field through the middle of the ruck, maul, scrum or lineout. The team which takes the ball across this imaginary line has for the moment gained the upper hand; by crossing the line, whether by one yard or by twenty, it has placed itself automatically on the attack, because the opposition must then move backwards to re-assemble its forces to counter the attack. Whatever a team's pattern or style of play, its prime objective must always be to cross the gain line.

Setting up the attack
The ideal scrum from which to attack is the one which is driving forward, or at least steady. The ball should be channelled quickly, usually to the no. 8's feet.

Such a scrum will normally be one into which your own scrum-half has put the ball, and it is essential that he has a thorough working knowledge of the laws relating to the scrum if he is not to give away penalties. He must also have complete understanding with his hooker as to the timing of his put-in. Proper co-ordination maximises the advantage of the put-in and avoids conceding unnecessary penalties as a result of mistiming. As there are more than fifty scrums in most games this co-ordination between scrum-half and hooker is vital. They must practise together their timing and a system of signals which will help their co-ordination.

If you are coming under pressure from the opposition drive on your put-in, all members of the back five in the scrum, and to a certain extent the props, put both feet right back. The knees are straightened and the feet splayed wide. If done properly, this position gives a strong static position which will enable the hooker to strike and the scrum-half to pick up the ball. Under pressure it is a very useful technique.

Attacking tactics from the set scrum
The objects are:

1. To gain ground quickly.
2. To tie in the opposing loose forwards and inside backs by forcing them to tackle.
3. To ensure continuity by good support.
4. To set up a ruck or maul in such a way that your side has the better chance of winning the ball from it.

The tactics you use to achieve these aims will depend on:

1. The position on the field of play of the scrum: in defence, in midfield, in attack or near your opponent's line; in the centre of the field, on the right-hand side or on the left-hand side; the amount of space available on the short side and the open side.
2. The scrummaging ability of both packs of forwards in terms of control, channelling and quality of possession.
3. The actions of the opposing team.
4. The ability of your back row and halves individually and as a unit.
5. The game plan.

Option 1. A quick ball to the fly-half to launch a handling, running, kicking attack. Ensure that the ball gets

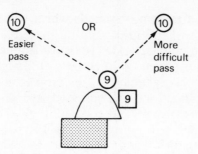

Attack from the set scrum: the pass to the fly-half

quickly to the no. 8's feet, preferably to his right so that his body will act as a shield against the menace of the opposing scrum-half. Loose forwards and scrum-half know which way the ball is going to be passed because of a pre-arranged signal, so they can initiate the attack and give support to the left or to the right.

Option 2. Attacking right. The no. 8 picks up going to his right. The scrum-half supports for a pass on his right,

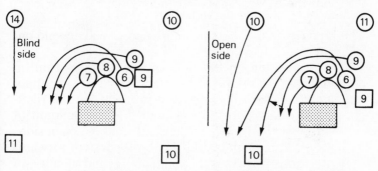

Attack from the set scrum: attacking right (1)

with the left-hand flanker coming round to give support. On the open side the scrum-half should aim for the opposing fly-half to try to set up an overlapping attack. On the blind side the attack should stay close to the scrum and the no. 8 should give a screen pass or short flip because of the limited space for the scrum-half to work in.

61

Option 3. Attacking right. The scrum-half feeds the no. 8, who has broken to the right of the scrum as the ball is being heeled. The attack develops as in option 2.

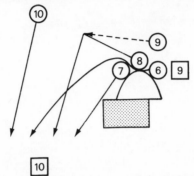

Attack from the set scrum: attacking right (2)

Option 4. Attacking left. The no. 8 picks up, passing to the scrum-half running to the left of the scrum. The no. 8 may be able to flick a quick pass or may have to drive into the opposing scrum-half before releasing the ball, depending on the actions of the opposing scrum-half.

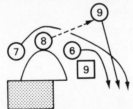

Attack from the set scrum: attacking left (1)

Option 5. Attacking left. The scrum-half or no. 8, depending on the actions of the opposing scrum-half, feeds

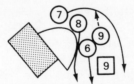

Attack from the set scrum: attacking left (2)

the right-hand flanker coming left. This is a particularly useful tactic against a pack which is deliberately wheeling your scrum.

Scrummaging variations

If the no. 8 packs between the left-hand flanker and left lock (moving one gap over), as Andie Leslie often did for the All Blacks, he can use his body as a shield to protect the

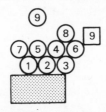

Scrummaging variations (1)

scrum-half. He can also start a handling attack a little quicker than normal by being in the channel through which it is most natural for the ball to emerge.

Packing 3-3-2 overloads the left-hand side of the scrum. The right flanker comes back to the no. 8's normal position, the no. 8 packing between the left flanker and left

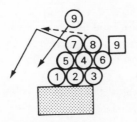

Scrummaging variations (2)

lock. The ball is channelled to the no. 8 who is well positioned to set up an attack on the left (options 4 and 5 above) or to flick a pass to the right-hand flanker breaking to the right of the scrum and supported by the scrum-half.

Coaching attack from the set scrum

Players should be made aware of the need to:

1. Know the alternatives at their disposal.
2. Use their strength and size to take out the opposing loose forwards immediately by driving close to the scrum and to make space for the support on the outside.
3. Use speed off the mark or a quick pass to launch the attack a little further away from the defending loose forwards.
4. Vary the type of pass in relation to the time available and the actions of the opposition, eg. screen pass, flip pass, lob pass, back flip etc.
5. Organise support depending on the actions of the ball carrier.
6. Time the support.
7. Understand what they are aiming to achieve and learn which moves they can use to the best advantage according to their own skills. This is something which the coach himself will also learn.

DEFENCE AT THE SET SCRUM

The eight-man shove

As the name implies, every forward plays his part in pushing back the opposition. This is not only good for morale, particularly early in a game, but if maintained it can ruin the opposition's play from the scrummage. The aims are:

1. To force the opposition into errors from which you may take advantage in counterattack.
2. To slow the heel down and thereby to stop the attack at source.
3. To slow down the scrum-half's pass to the fly-half by making it more difficult to get away.
4. To stop all back-row attacks.
5. To place the fly-half under pressure.

Tight binding is essential, and after the scrum has gone down extra pressure can be exerted on the opposition by trying to bind even more tightly. The knees of the forwards are bent to give a good springboard for the dynamic drive when the ball comes in. The whole scrum also tries to go that shade lower when it goes down. A gradual build-up of pressure is exerted on the opposition and on the call of the leader (not necessarily the pack leader) the knees snap straight, the bottom sinks, the shoulders thrust forward and the scrum moves towards the opposition's line. This pressure must be maintained, which is normally quite easy; once the opposition begin to go back it is very difficult for them to reassert themselves and the speed of retreat can even be increased. This is a scrum-half's nightmare.

The right-hand side of the scrum is defended by the scrum-half harrying his opponent and forcing him into errors. The right-hand flank forward breaks forward as soon as the ball emerges to take advantage of any errors by the opposing scrum-half or to pressure any receiver on his side of the scrum. Similarly, the left-hand flank forward pincers on the scrum-half, or moves quickly onto any receiver on his side of the scrum, supported by the no. 8.

The wheel
If the opposition pack is good enough to resist an eight-man shove, an alternative weapon is the wheel. Here, the object is to spin the scrum so rapidly that the opposition lose control of the ball. There are a number of ways in which it can be done, but normally it will be a clockwise movement: ie. the loose head goes forward and the tight head goes back. Scrums have a natural tendency to spin like this, and so it is just a question of accelerating the effect. The tight-head prop, right-hand lock and flanker all pull as the ball comes into the scrum, while the rest of the pack drives hard. If it is done well, a spinning scrum develops from which it becomes extremely difficult for the opposition to clear the ball. Many different ways have been tried to counter this move, but providing it is

used sparingly it invariably disrupts the opposition.

The scrum-half challenges hard for the ball on the right-hand side of the scrum, always keeping his feet behind the ball. The right flanker breaks back behind the scrummage off-side line (the back foot of the scrum), moving to his right at the same time. He is then able to support his scrum-half quickly when the ball emerges, either to take advantage of opposition mistakes or to stop any attacks down that side. The left-hand flanker pincers on the opposing scrum-half or no. 8, or goes for the interception of any pass to the fly-half or other receiver on his side of the scrum. He may be able to tackle the receiver, man and ball. He must think quickly and act accordingly, remembering to keep firmly bound as the scrum wheels and to break forward as soon as, but not before, the ball is out. The no. 8 may support his flanker on the left-hand side if the ball emerges on that side, or give extra support on the right to his scrum-half and right-hand flanker should the opponents bring the ball down that side. He thinks, uses his judgement and acts accordingly.

The scrum-half
The scrum-half should know when his side is going to attempt a definite eight-man shove or a deliberate wheel as this will help him to position himself to attack his opposite number or, as is often the case these days, the no. 8. He must also be aware that the channelling of the opposing scrum may not always be good, particularly when his own hooker and tight-head prop are putting their opposition under pressure; in these circumstances the ball will often shoot out at the side of the scrum. His aim should be to stop possession at source by catching his opponent with the ball or at least stopping him getting it away cleanly. A good spoiling scrum-half is of great value to his side as he can force his opponent into errors by his pressure. It is important that the scrum-half should keep his feet behind the ball, but always go either for the ball as soon as it is out of the scrummage or for his opponent's arms.

Defensive tactics at the set scrum

Assuming that the ball has arrived safely with the opposing scrum-half, the main aims of the forwards, particularly the back row, are now:

1. To force the opposition into errors by aggressive defence.
2. To be ready to capitalise on any mistakes made as a result.
3. To stop the opposing attack at source by a pressing defence, which forces the opponents to play the game behind the gain line.
4. To prevent breaks close to the scrum by the opposing scrum-half and loose forwards, covering each other as necessary.
5. To prevent the opposing fly-half from penetrating.
6. To prevent any penetration from scissors between the opposing threequarters.
7. To cover across the field as near to the ball as possible.
8. To win every breakdown wherever it occurs by being there first.

The way in which these aims are achieved will be decided by similar considerations to those which affect the choice of attacking tactics – see page 60.

Close to the scrum. Against a loose-forward and scrum-half attack the basic defence is two men either side of the scrum, right flanker and scrum-half on the right, left flanker and no. 8 on the left. The fly-half takes his own man but is also prepared to tackle any ball carrier coming at him. Attacks are more likely to be launched down the left-hand side as it is the natural way to go with the ball being put in on the loose head. The left-hand flanker must be prepared to anticipate the move, get in position and tackle head-on whenever he can to stop the opponents crossing the gain line. The no. 8 must also be able to break quickly to support the left flanker's action, taking the

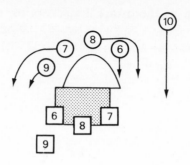

Defence close to the scrum

second man round whether on the outside or the inside of the flanker. If an attack should come down the right-hand side close to the scrum, the scrum-half takes the first man and the right flanker acts like the no. 8 on the other side, taking the second man round.

Further from the scrum. If on the left-hand side, the left-hand flanker will make sure that the ball has been passed, then move quickly after the ball and the fly-half or any other receiver, aiming to tackle him in possession wherever

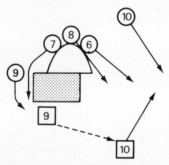

Defence further from the scrum

possible. The no. 8 will cover first the inside, taking the fly-half should he manage to beat the left-hand flanker and step back inside. He should watch for the fly-half changing the direction of the attack by scissoring with either his centre or his full-back, or by simply passing to the blind-side wing. Second, the no. 8 will cover close to the ball to be first or second to the breakdown and win the tackled ball; the full-back and both wings should be looking after the deeper cover. On the right-hand side, the right-hand flanker similarly goes for the receiver of the opposing scrum-half's pass, which should in any case have been hampered by the determined challenge of his own scrum-half. The no. 8 behaves exactly as for an attack down the other side but will check first that there is no danger on the left-hand side of the scrum; the flanker going for the fly-half should be aware of this and of the possibility of his no. 8 not being in quite such a good position to take the fly-half should he jink inside.

9

The Lineout

'The lineouts were messy' – how often one hears this criticism of games at all levels. Despite the various efforts made by the administrators the standard of lineout play generally has not improved and it is a long way from fulfilling its function as a means of supplying clean, good ball. The best, or most controlled, lineout ball was supplied in the days when double banking was legal, but sadly, this is no longer the case. Another means of improving lineout possession has been to develop a lifting technique, but this too is illegal. The present laws demand that players must stand one behind the other with a space of at least one metre between them and separated by a space of half a metre from the opposition. The theory behind these spaces is that it encourages the clean, two-handed catch, but unfortunately it inhibits the support and has not significantly improved lineout play.

Of course the game must be played according to the laws in force at the time, but it will not have escaped many that in most lineouts the jumper tends to deflect, not catch, and that he deflects with the outside hand. The inside arm must be doing something and it is usually fending off his opponent. Outside-hand deflection is almost by definition illegal but it still occurs in game after game. If it is every man for himself, as it appears to be, why does the law not appreciate this?

Despite these reservations the lineout can, with diligent practice, become a useful and even vital source of ball. No side can hope to win many games without at least one very good lineout forward; most sides have three jumpers, some less and some lucky sides more. In the context of the lineout, obviously the more good jumpers a side has the better because this gives more options or more alternatives. For example, in a side with three jumpers the standard positions for them are two, four and six (assuming a seven-man lineout with a member of the front row throwing in), but too many sides stick rigidly to this formation. A number of different combinations are possible. Why not have jumpers together at two and three, or four and six? Why not put all three jumpers together at three, four and five? Each side has to work out the best arrangement for itself but beware of inflexibility.

THE THROW

The most important player in the lineout is the thrower. This has often been said but it is no less true for all that. Most throwers are poor and until there is a general improvement in this skill there will be no improvement in general lineout play. Most teams now use the hooker as their thrower but this should never be taken as the only answer; if one accepts the importance of the throw then obviously the best thrower should do the job. In fact, the choice of thrower normally comes down to one of the front row. At London Welsh in the late 'sixties, both flankers, John Taylor and Tony Gray, were persuaded to try throwing. They were both good but both complained bitterly that they could not get into the game again quickly enough. So the throwing job usually ends up back with the hooker but here is an example of wrong priorities: selectors are probably more to blame than most in this respect.

Of the various techniques of throwing only one deserves consideration: the torpedo throw. Its flexibility is enormous, as shown by American football. It can be used to throw fast or slow, high or low, and the thrower should be capable of performing each type of throw equally well. One way in which he can improve is by simply throwing

5 Delme Thomas has missed this throw for Wales against France in 1972, but Mervyn Davies covers the danger. A good example of reacting to a situation.

along the goal line at a goal post, aiming to hit it at different heights and speeds. This practice must be done regularly so that in a game the thrower can put the ball in just the right place. He must also be able to throw straight, which is particularly difficult in the case of the extremely long throw over the top of the lineout. The idea is for the back man to retreat and then to deflect or catch the ball, or it can go even further to the scrum-half running round. This throw can be very effective, particularly if the back man is reasonably quick. It was a bonus which London Welsh and Wales enjoyed for many years thanks to the combination of Mervyn Davies and John Taylor. Most sides were so busy marking and attempting to upset Mervyn that quite frequently 'wee John Taylor' could win a lot of ball.

Wherever the throw is being aimed, its speed, trajectory and height must be known to the thrower, all the forwards and the scrum-half.

THE CATCH

There are two basic types of throw for any position in the lineout, the fast throw and the slower, more lobbed throw. Each requires a different catching technique.

The fast, flat throw

The fast throw is normally thrown lower and, particularly at the front and the middle of the line, it is easier to catch cleanly because there is less time for the opposition to interfere. Catching this type of throw is a specialised technique. The jumper must attack the ball, normally jumping forwards and inwards as well as upwards. If the timing is good catching should be perfectly easy, with the outside hand clamping onto the ball as soon as it has been stopped by the inside hand. Once you have made the catch, every effort should be made to turn your back to the opposition and thus protect the ball. In fact, the best exponents are turning just before they catch the ball, giving their opponents even less time to react.

Having caught it, you have the choice of two ways of delivering the ball. The best is to bring it down very quickly and then to pass it to the scrum-half when he wants it. Provided the support play is effective this technique should ensure clear delivery. The other technique is more risky but can be used now and again. Instead of bringing the ball down, the jumper throws the ball to his scrum-half from the top of his leap. This second method seldom works very well at the highest level but can be very useful if one jumper is much better than his opposite number.

6 Chris Howcroft makes a good two-handed catch despite Chris Ralston's attentions. The player behind Howcroft (Ed Powell) has not moved quickly enough to support him. Richmond v. London Welsh, 1977.

The slow, lobbed throw

The same basic principles apply to the lobbed throw but catching here is more difficult as the opposition has more time to compete for the ball. It takes a very good lineout forward to catch throws of this type consistently. Delme Thomas could do it but he sometimes had a little assistance!

Deflecting

Deflecting the ball is the alternative to catching. Notice the term 'deflecting', which implies control, not 'tapping', which has an uncontrolled sound. This technique requires the ball to be guided from the top of the leap to the receiver. It must be done accurately and not wildly, and more scrum-halves have suffered nightmares from wild tapping

7 Chris Ralston controls this deflection. Where has his opponent gone? Richmond v. London Welsh, 1977.

75

than from anything else. Ball tapped badly is often ball not worth winning – if only the reporters who assess a team's lineout performance on the number of times they tap the ball in the general direction of their own goal line were scrum-halves!

The master deflector was Mervyn Davies, who had the uncanny knack of guiding the ball to the right place while being subjected to all manner of obstruction. In fact his contribution to Welsh and Lions rugby was based to a large degree on this ability – though he could also do other things quite well! Deflecting really means getting the hand round and over the ball and directing it gently downwards. The deflection can be to the scrum-half or, as is now quite common, to another forward in the lineout who is acting as a buffer. He takes the job of clearing up and, when two lineout sides are evenly balanced, this is an extremely valuable way of protecting the scrum-half.

THE PEEL

The peel round the back

This is probably the best known alternative to delivering the ball direct to the scrum-half from the lineout. The French and the New Zealanders are past-masters at it. It is essentially a long throw, followed by a deflection to a forward bursting round from the front of the lineout.

The throw must be accurate and preferably to the last but one man in the line. This allows the last man to act as a safety net if the throw goes too far or to be actively involved in support if the throw is true. If the thrower is not certain he can hit the exact spot he should always aim to throw too far rather than too short; the too long throw can be tidied up by the last man but the shorter one will probably be picked off by the opposition.

Two people should be nominated to follow the ball round at first. The receiver follows a path close to the lineout and when he receives the ball he should immediately aim to swing around towards the opposition's post. He must *not* run across the field. As soon as he meets the opposition he either hands the ball on to a supporting player or sets up a ruck or maul. The receiver must have the ability to judge which of the two alternatives is the right one.

The second man should take up a slightly wider arc and

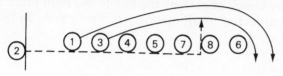

Lineout peel round the back

his job is to tidy up any situation. For example, if the deflection should go over the receiver's head the second man must be able to retrieve the situation, but if the deflection is accurate he is in a good position to support the receiver. The other players then pile round the back of the ball carrier in as close a formation as possible. It is unlikely against a good defence that the carrier will get very far forward, and if he is stopped they must be on hand to carry on the drive or to win the ensuing ruck or maul.

Defence against the peel round the back of the line depends initially on anticipation and on putting the jumper under pressure. The player at the back of the lineout is responsible for attacking the first opponent to receive the ball from the jumper. He must avoid attempts to obstruct him and must aim to tackle the receiver on the other side of the gain line. Forwards from the front of the lineout shadow their opponents to the back of the line and prevent them from breaking forward.

The peel round the front
The ball is thrown to the first jumper who, having caught it, passes it to a man coming round from the back of the line. This is a good variation and can even produce a score if used close to the opponents' line. The thrower must support the move instantly.

77

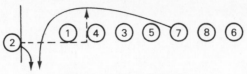

Lineout peel round the front

For the defence, the player in the five-metre area (their ball) or the thrower-in, plus the front player in the lineout, are responsible for preventing breaks around the front. The loose forwards in particular must accept responsibility for covering their opponents in drives around the front. Anticipate, watch out for signals, and cover.

THE SHORTENED LINEOUT

These have gained in popularity and the best exponents are probably the Japanese. What they lack in height they make up for by their speed of thought and foot. It is a good ploy for any side whose forwards are being subjected to excessive harassment in the normal lineout, as the absence of too many interfering opponents enables them to use their ability to better value. Two-, three- and four-man lines are all used and several different moves can be executed from these mini-lineouts.

For example, from a two-man lineout in which the ball is deflected to the scrum-half by the back man, instead of passing to his fly-half the scrum-half pivots and throws a pass to a forward steaming up in the five-metre area.

Another tactic is to throw the ball over the top of the line to the scrum-half, who runs flat across the field doing a dummy scissors with both fly-half and inside centre before doing a scissors with a flanker running hard down the middle of the field.

In some shortened lineouts it can be an advantage to have a forward standing in the position normally occupied by the scrum-half. Several sides do this and, provided the forward is carefully selected, he can play a significant part in setting up attacks.

LINEOUT SUPPORT PLAY

Although each member of the lineout is a potential ball winner and must keep his eyes on the ball, some members have more of a supporting than a directly ball winning role.

The easiest and most efficient support depends on a catch. As soon as the ball is caught each forward has a specific part to play. Players in front and behind must immediately isolate the catcher from the opposition, and there are two good ways of doing this: the first is for both supporters to bind quickly around the waist of the jumper; alternatively, both drive past the jumper with their shoulders while binding securely to the jumper's shirt, and provided they keep their feet back there is no reason why they should not do this. Either type of support prevents interference from nearby opponents but the remaining opponents must also be prevented from running through the lineout. The legal way to prevent this is for each man to bind onto his nearest team-mate, thus setting up a maul. It is now very difficult for the opposition to lay a hand on the ball. Often a man is delegated from the catcher's own side to take the ball from him, thus further isolating the opposition. This person must stay close to the line of the lineout. The variations possible in this type of support play are legion and each side must work out its own method, which must be both legal and effective. Any illegal method, while possibly working for a couple of games, will eventually be recognised and penalised. If the team has no alternative plan then the opposition will have a field day.

The last man in the lineout is usually exempt from this sort of support work. He will break backwards if his side has won the ball to get into a good position to support the backs if they are given the ball, or the scrum-half if he makes a break.

It is more difficult to support the jumper who is deflecting the ball. The major problem that sides must recognise is the legal one. No player may move until the ball has been touched, so if the support players obey this law the ball is already travelling in the direction of the scrum-half.

If the deflection is accurate, all well and good, but if it is wild the opposition can pour through and give the scrum-half a miserable time. There is no satisfactory way of over-coming this problem unless one uses illegal ploys such as 'compression'. This involves all the players on the jumper's side moving towards the jumper and sideways towards the opposition. This technique has been used effectively by a number of sides but it is still illegal. Deflecting to a support man in the lineout is one way out of the difficulty but it does slow down significantly the release of the ball.

When three forwards stand together in the middle of a lineout and all jump for the ball this automatically affords more protection. It also gives the thrower more scope for error. The disadvantage of this approach is that it limits the alternatives available to the throwing side.

DEFENCE AT THE LINEOUT

As soon as the ball leaves the line, the players outside the lineout should aim to narrow the twenty-metre gap as quickly as possible. Meanwhile the players within the line-out try to break forward and put the opposition under as much pressure as possible, particularly the scrum-half. In fact, unless the opposition are using the peel, it is their halves on whom you should concentrate your defensive pressure. The last player in the lineout challenges the fly-half as quickly as possible. He has to use his judgement to assess the quality of possession: if the ball is being tapped he should be off the tail of the lineout in a flash, aiming to split the half-backs or to arrive on the fly-half as he receives the ball. The second man from the end takes the scrum-half should he elect to run, and provides cover quickly if he passes. The rest of the lineout players aim to put pressure on the scrum-half whenever they can get through. They must all be flexible and alive to the loose ball.

10

Forward Play in the Loose

ARRIVING AT THE BREAKDOWN

The forward who arrives first at the loose ball after a breakdown has a number of alternatives, and he will judge which to adopt depending on the circumstances. He can:

1. Fall on the ball to stop an opposition drive, aiming to get back on his feet as quickly as possible.
2. Ruck over the top, staying on his feet.
3. Pick up the ball and feed it at once to his support.
4. Pick up the ball and drive down the field with the ball in his hands.
5. Screen the ball and set up a maul.

He chooses for the rest of the forwards who give him the appropriate support for whichever option he has decided on. The quality of the support determines the length of your team's possession of the ball, the number of passes that can be strung together, the quality of ball from the next ruck or maul and even, as will be seen, who puts the ball into the next scrum. It provides continuity by giving the ball carrier more than one direction in which to feed the ball, from set pieces as well as in broken play. Quick support is also essential to effective mauling and rucking. Forwards must learn to anticipate play when not immediately concerned and should always be working hard 'off the ball' to get into a position to support. Good support depends on attitude, skill and fitness.

CLOSE HANDLING AND PASSING

As with all passing, the idea is to give the ball to the supporting player who is in a better position to make use of it, but in close play particular care must be taken to ensure that the ball is transferred surely, giving the opposition as little opportunity as possible to interfere. The basic idea is to commit an opponent fully by driving into him and then releasing the ball to the support.

Body position
The key to successful contact is the right body position, leaning forward from the waist at about forty-five degrees with the back straight. Jim Wallace, a former All Black

8 An aggressive drive by Derek Quinnell during the Jubilee Match, Lions v Barbarians, at Twickenham in 1977. Notice how Quinnell leans forward (Mike Knill is soon to feel the impact) and how Gordon Brown and Bill Beaumont are in close support.

coach, says 'Why do we lean forward? It is the most effective way to drive into a ruck or maul; to bind onto a fellow forward; to accept a pop-up; and to be able to search for the ball on the ground or in a maul.' It makes pretty good sense, especially as it is also much harder to tackle a leaner than it is to stop an upright runner.

Contact

Where should the ball carrier aim to make contact with the defender? If the tackler is standing upright he is extremely vulnerable and the carrier should aim to drive his leading shoulder into his opponent's stomach or lower chest. If the immediate effect is to crumple the defender then the carrier can run on. If however the ball carrier senses sterner stuff he should now immediately present the ball to his support.

All forwards must become expert at contact skills as ball carriers, support players and ball winners. The three principles for the ball carrier to remember are:

1. Hit him harder than he hits you.
2. Think of the position of the ball.
3. Think of where your support is coming from.

Making the ball available

When the ball carrier approaches his would-be tackler he must ensure that the ball is kept available. Most forwards hold the ball in their right arm and attack the tackler with the left arm and shoulder. This is a satisfactory method provided the ball carrier is able to distribute the ball immediately and keeps it well away from the tackler.

When should the ball carrier try to adopt a position which makes it easier for him to release the ball? When we in the UK began to try to emulate the New Zealanders at this aspect of play we got it all wrong. So many times one would see the ball carrier leaning forward in the approved style but as soon as he came to within a couple of yards of the tackler he would accomplish a clumsy pirouette and then try to reverse into the tackler. This took away his prime advantage, his controlled momentum. By the time he reached the tackler he was either going so slowly that he did not fully commit the defender, or going backwards so uncontrollably that it was easy for him to be thrown to the ground and robbed of the ball.

The secret of this skill is to make contact and then to make the ball available to the support. This commits the defender fully and, if the tackle is weak, the ball carrier can drive through and so gain more ground.

Supposing, though, that the ball carrier has opted to hand the ball on to his support, this can be done in two ways. One approach follows the New Zealand pattern, the other is essentially European.

New Zealand. When contact is made, or perhaps just before, the ball is transferred from the arm to the trailing hip. The ball is thus well away from the tackler and, provided support is quick to arrive, the ball can be snatched away and the drive downfield continued. The carrier must try to stay on his feet until after the ball has been carried on. If he does not do so he will end up in an undignified heap on the ground, unable to pass the ball on effectively.

European. As soon as tough resistance is felt the ball carrier must make a violent effort to turn so that he can now see his support. This is done by wrenching the upper portion of the body half round and by holding the ball away from the opposition. The next player then takes the ball and continues the drive. A modification of this technique is for the ball carrier, when he sees the support, to lob the ball to him rather than just holding it. The support player should be trying to get close to the carrier, so it is important that the pass should be no more than a lob; many times one sees the ball go to ground because the pass has been far too hard. Like every other ball transfer, this demands complete co-operation between the giver and the receiver.

The European method has two major advantages over the New Zealand style. First, it enables the ball carrier to see his support and so to make decisions regarding the distance they have to run to support him. The New Zealand method banks on the immediate presence in the right place of the support, which is an admirable ideal but one that is not always met. The second advantage of the European method is that when the tackle is effective, if the carrier has adopted the New Zealand style he now has no efficient means of transferring the ball. He dives into the ground with the ball still on his hip and when he meets the ground the ball is out of his control. On the other hand, the carrier using the European style has time when tackled to transfer the ball. Here it must be remembered that if the ball does not touch the ground no tackle has been made and the player can still pass the ball legally. So when the tackle is made the ball carrier must make every effort to roll so that when he hits the ground he is on his back with the ball held up. He can now wait for his support to take the ball from him or he can pop the ball up for the attack to continue.

Although not normally renowned for his charging drives, the best example of keeping the ball available after a tackle in this way is Gerald Davies. Even when tackled from the side he usually manages to turn and pass on the ball as he hits the ground.

Support
Up to now, this section has focused only on the ball carrier. The other person vitally involved is of course the receiver. Although the major responsibility is on the carrier or distributor, the receiver must also play his part if the transfer is to be successful and the movement carried on. He must:

1. Position himself three to four yards behind the ball carrier so that when the ball carrier wishes to transfer the ball he can see the support arriving.
2. Adopt the leaning forward, running style, as when he takes the ball he is likely to come into contact with

the opposition very quickly, and will be more easily stopped if he is in the upright position.

3. Attack the ball by accelerating into it. If a support player slows down to take the ball all momentum disappears and the drive peters out. He must also wrench the ball away from the carrier and not hold his hands out in the hope that the ball will stick there. If the ball is popped up to him he must still concentrate (that word again) on accelerating while keeping his eyes firmly on the ball.

If the receiver remembers these three major points he is more likely to carry on the attack and drive towards the opposition line. There are few more fearsome sights than a pack on the rampage in this type of close support play.

THE RUCK

'New Zealanders are the best ruckers in the world.' Very few people would disagree with this statement. Their approach to rucking is very simple: if the ball is on the ground they drive straight over it and leave the ball behind for their scrum-half. If someone is wrapped around the ball they drive straight over him and the ball, leaving both for their scrum-half.

The ruck, although not as controllable as a maul, is still a vital weapon in any pack's armoury. Packs can become too committed to rucking to the exclusion of all else, but if done properly at the proper time it can be a crucial ball supplier. It is vitally important that when the forwards arrive at a breakdown they know whether they are going to ruck or maul the ball back. If some try to ruck and others to

9 *(opposite, above)*. Peter Dixon makes the ball available to his support with a one-handed pass during the final England trial in 1974. This unorthodox technique can be very effective.

10 *(opposite, below)*. Despite being tackled by two Irishmen during the 1975 international, Gerald Davies still keeps the ball available.

maul the result is confusion, but the decision is usually straightforward: if the ball is in the hand a maul should normally develop, if on the ground it should be rucked. Even so there are exceptions to these general principles. If the first player to a breakdown has time to pick up the ball then obviously he should do so. As ever, good judgement is essential.

If a player driving forward with the ball is successfully tackled and cannot continue the movement by slipping the ball up to a support player, then this is the ideal set-up for a ruck. The tackled player must bear one thing in mind: if he falls so that his back is to his own players it makes it far more difficult for an effective ruck to develop. He must fall so that his back is to the opposition and the ball nearer to his team-mates. This should happen automatically if he is concentrating on trying to turn to give the ball to his support.

The forwards should aim to arrive at the breakdown as a unit, for no good rucking can be done by players who turn up in ones or twos. Inevitably, though, there will be a slight time-lag between the first and last arrivals, and the first forwards to reach the fallen player must bind tightly together, adopt the leaning position and drive into the opposition so that they pass over the ball. The old term for a ruck was a loose scrum and although this term does not adequately fill the bill, the same basic principles apply as to a set scrum: the binding must be tight, the body position must be low and the intention must be to drive the opposition backwards.

The forwards arriving first at the ruck must also strain to stay on their feet. There is no way in which the forward drive can be maintained if they do not, since supporters arriving at high speed will also fall over. Too many British rucks end up with a pile of bodies on the ground.

Once the first forwards have established a platform the later arrivals must have one thought and one thought only: to drive the opposition back so quickly that the ball is available for the scrum-half. To do this they too must bind onto a colleague as they approach the ruck, and drive in low and hard onto the rumps of the first forwards. Having started the opposition retreat they must keep it up by pumping their legs hard.

Every forward must keep his eyes open as he enters the ruck. The ball is too often kicked away as a result of some well-intentioned idiot charging into the ruck with his eyes closed. There should be no need for any forward actually to touch the ball with his feet, and in fact, he should be actively discouraged from doing so. If the drive is fierce enough then the forwards will just run over the ball. A stationary ball waits for the scrum-half, making his task considerably easier.

One problem with the ruck is the opportunity it gives for indiscriminate use of the boot. Although they should have no truck with this approach, a certain amount of sympathy can be felt for a good rucking side who are countered by unlawful defensive work. The most common example of this is a player holding onto the ball after a tackle. Consider this situation: a garryowen is hoisted and is taken by the opposition's full-back. He is immediately tackled to the ground but instead of releasing the ball he holds onto it. The oncoming pack have very little option but to drive over him, quite possibly treading on him in the process. The full-back has no one to blame but himself, as killing the ball in the ruck is one of the most dangerous and provocative acts in rugby. It is sometimes difficult for referees to see clearly but they should be the prime movers in stamping it out by adhering strictly to the law.

THE MAUL

In the last few years there has been an increasing emphasis in British rugby on the maul. When the New Zealanders of the 'sixties came to Britain their strong point was their rucking ability. Many sides tried to emulate them with varying degrees of success but gradually it was realised that the ball in the hand was more controllable than the ball on the ground. As a result, a considerable amount of thought has gone into ensuring quality possessions from mauls.

The set maul

There are several types of maul and each one requires a slightly different technique. The set maul can crop up many times in a game, but the best example is when a side is receiving a kick-off. The basics of this situation are:

1. The catcher must call for the ball early. Too often either two men go for the ball at the kick-off or

11 The ball is well protected from the opposition in this maul during Stanley's Match at Oxford in 1975, but the players should be tighter together – no doubt they would be for Pontypool!

nobody does. Having called and then caught the ball, the catcher now makes every effort to turn his back on the opposition immediately so that he protects the ball. As well as turning he must also spread his feet apart and lower his body into a strong, resistant position.

2. The two players on either side of the catcher must move to support him as soon as he moves towards the ball. They must not bind before he catches the ball but once he has it in his hands they must be in very quickly. If the support on either side of the catcher is not fast enough then all his good work is worth nothing: the opposition can quickly isolate him from his team-mates and the ball will be lost. The immediate support players bind on either side of the catcher, over his back to isolate the ball even more efficiently from the opposition. The binding must be tight, and care must be taken that the referee does not confuse the legitimate binding with obstruction.

3. The next player into the maul immediately drives low into the catcher and, while maintaining close contact with him, takes the ball. He must attack the ball and not passively wait to be handed it. If this aspect of the maul is well done the opposition even by this time should have very little chance of getting their hands on the ball. The new ball carrier must also adopt the low, feet apart stance.

4. The next players to arrive also have a specific role to play. They take up binding positions on the first two support players so that a wedge shape is formed. The ball is now so well protected that the scrum-half calls for it only when he is ready.

This type of maul is comparatively easy to control and is similar to the lineout (page 79). There, if the catcher does his job, the rest of the players have functions very like those in the set maul.

One note of caution: too many mauls take too long

91

because too many people want to get their hands on the ball. Two people and two people only are enough for the proper transfer of the ball to the scrum-half. The forward who, trying to impress the selectors, gets his hands to the ball needlessly is not only being unhelpful, he is actually hindering his own side.

The moving maul

When a player running forwards with the ball is tackled he cannot always transfer the ball safely and directly to a supporting player to carry on the movement. This often happens when a centre tries to take a crash ball through the opposition defence. When this type of situation develops the best way of keeping the movement going is to set up a moving maul.

When the tackle is made the ball carrier must make every effort to remain on his feet, turn and adopt the low, feet apart stance. The first player in support now has two options. He can drive past the carrier, binding over him as he does so and effectively isolating one side of the ball carrier. If the support arrives quickly the next man binds on the other side of the carrier, the next man takes the ball and the maul develops just as in the set maul.

Alternatively, if the first support player judges that he is well ahead of his colleagues, and that one side of the ball carrier will therefore remain vulnerable, he drives into the ball carrier instead of past him, and takes the ball from him. If there is no opposition close at hand he makes off with the ball. If there is opposition, he adopts the turned, low, feet apart stance. He has thus removed the ball from the immediate danger area. The support, on arriving, now drives past the new ball carrier, again forming the wedge and isolating the ball from the opposition.

Both techniques have their advantages and the choice of the right one depends on the circumstances. Usually either a flanker or another back is first to arrive at this type of situation and he must make the right decision. This obviously means that backs must be able to maul, and the success of Welsh international rugby in recent years has been in no small way due to the mauling ability of their backs.

The retreating maul

Mauling, like most other features of forward play, is easy going forwards. It is far more difficult on the retreat. Typically, a retreating maul develops when a kick is put through by the opposition and the full-back is caught in possession. The nearest player must go in and take the ball from the full-back, thus giving the forwards time to arrive at the breakdown. He too must stick to the basic principle of turning and taking a low, feet apart position. The arriving forwards must now go round behind the new carrier and in their turn carry out the operations needed to form the wedge. They must arrive quickly, otherwise the opposition will easily drive through.

For a forward, this is probably the most demanding job, both physically and psychologically, that he has to do. A good forward shows his worth not only by being quick to the breakdown going forward but equally quick to the breakdown when on the retreat.

The stalemate maul

Despite intensive coaching many mauls end up in a huffing, puffing group of players achieving very little. It is inevitable that sometimes you will not set up a neat, organised maul but rather a struggling mass of players. One of the techniques that has been developed to end this stalemate is for a player close to the ball to use his full weight to try to release it. He can push down while wrenching away from the opposition. This is the most common method used by the best maulers. Another technique demands co-operation between players. If an opponent is holding the ball tightly one player takes the right arm away from the ball while another player takes the left away. A third player then rips the ball out and is in a position to feed. Yet another approach that may be used is for one of the players

93

struggling for the ball to drop to the ground and thus use all his body weight for pulling the ball from the opposition. Brian Thomas (Neath and Wales) used this technique very successfully to become one of the best maulers in the game.

If these and other methods fail to release the ball a scrum will be called by the referee, and the team going forward will get the put-in. This is another reason why it is important for only a couple of players to be involved in the struggle for the ball, while their team-mates concentrate on driving the maul towards the opposition's line.

TACTICS AT RUCK AND MAUL

The tactical approach should be flexible as each ruck or maul develops at different times and in different positions on the field. It may be the first after a set piece with the defence fairly settled, or it may be the last in a series of several rucks and mauls, when it is more difficult to organise both the defence and the attack.

Attack

Ball won from the ruck or maul must be moved quickly; if it has emerged with little delay it is usually worth attacking in the same direction, but if the ball is slow, try switching direction. If in doubt attack the short side, which is often less well defended.

As well as the scrum-half break or the pass to the fly-half to start a handling movement by the backs, other options are:

1. The scrum-half pops the ball up to a forward who has hung back and is now running hard, straight down the field close to the ruck or maul. The regions close to the ruck or maul are often poorly defended and he can make tremendous inroads into the defenders' territory.
2. A big forward rolls away from a maul, or picks up the ball as it emerges from a ruck, and carries on the

94

drive; Derek Quinnell is a good exponent of this. It quite often gives a forward the opportunity to run directly at the opposition fly-half, a development not normally appreciated by the fly-half, and it can lead to a big thrust down the field. This peeling is sometimes overdone but kept within reason it can be a very effective ploy.

Defence

An opposing ball carrier's task of setting up a successful ruck or maul is made much harder if the tackler both prevents him from passing the ball to one of his supporters and turns him in the tackle so that the opponent's back is between the ball and his support. Despite having to

12 Derek Quinnell, playing for the Lions against Nelson-Bays in 1977, drives off a maul. Note his low body position and the close support which Squire, Beaumont, Windsor and Price are ready to give.

re-group behind the ball, the tackler's forwards then have an excellent chance of regaining the ball if they remember the basic techniques of rucking and mauling.

As a general rule the scrum-half can defend the short side of a ruck or maul and the last forward can look after the open side. Some people hold that this smacks of defeatism and that the extra momentum of this last player could be all that is needed finally to drive the opposition back. It can certainly be argued that all players approaching an attacking ruck or maul must play their full part, but in defence it can be very worthwhile for the last forward to stand out and prevent the scrum-half from breaking along the short side. This technique was used by the 1971 Lions in New Zealand and it helped to stifle Sid Going's running.

The number of players allocated to defend each side may in fact vary with circumstances, and communication between players becomes particularly important.

11

The Scrum-Half

The modern scrum-half is a highly skilled technician. His skills are based upon certain natural qualities, both physical and mental. To the physical qualities of speed, strength and stamina, the extra qualities of good balance, agility, quick reactions and resilience must be added; as well as the mental qualities of concentration, confidence and judgement he needs alertness, awareness, adaptability, speed of thought, the competitive spirit and great courage. These natural qualities form a basic structure upon which a scrum-half may build his repertoire of specialist skills and techniques. The scrum-half's position on the field of play, close to his forwards, makes heavy demands upon his skills and attitude, and it is essential that he acts quickly, decisively and with courage. The best player available must always be chosen in this vital position.

Recent developments in the game have increased the scope of scrum-half play. The changes in the off-side law relating to scrum, lineout, ruck and maul, and the change in forward play as a result of better coaching, have improved the quality of possession, which he must use wisely. The introduction of the spin pass has enabled him to adopt a standing position behind his forwards from which he may launch a handling, running or kicking attack. He is better able as a result to use his vision and natural footballing ability to influence the course of the game, either by posing a threat or by dictating tactics. It is important, therefore, that he should have sound mental qualities – knowledge of the game, experience and a natural gift for tactics. His

13 Gareth Edwards uses all his speed, strength and determination to force the break as he storms at the All Black defence with this match-winning run for the British Lions in the Third Test at Wellington in 1971. Bob Burgess lifts off as he is pushed aside by the power of the hand-off which enabled Gareth to set up Barry John for a vital score.

judgement and appreciation of the different situations in the game is the key to the team's success.

Gareth Edwards displays all the qualities required of the modern scrum-half: speed and length of pass, superb running ability, outstanding capabilities as a kicker, allied to an ability to read the game and to make correct decisions. But he has also brought a new dimension to modern scrum-half play. His speed of pass is an essential part of his make-up, and to Chris Laidlaw's spin pass he has added his own pivot pass which he uses from lineouts, particularly on the left of the field, to fire the ball enormous distances. To Clive Rowlands' kicking skills he has developed his own long torpedo kick, which he uses to establish position from the scrum, ruck and maul; he performs this kick with amazing accuracy and has an uncanny knack of being able to bounce the ball into touch. To Sid Going's running skills he has added his own brand of determination and athleticism; in attacking running he has no equal, and his natural speed means that he can score as easily from seventy metres as five metres. But even to these outstanding individual skills he adds something extra: he is a magnificent team player who realises the importance of his role in the team plan, and this quality, combined with superb judgement and a fierce competitive spirit, makes him a model scrum-half.

THE PASSING SCRUM-HALF

Examples
During the nineteen-thirties, Danie Craven, the famous Springbok, revolutionised scrum-half passing by introducing the dive pass to the international scene. His example was quickly followed by others and the dive pass soon became an essential for all scrum-halves. Indeed all the famous British Lions scrum-halves – Haydn Tanner, Rex Willis, Dickie Jeeps, Andie Mulligan, Alan Lewis and Roger Young – were expert at passing great distances with the dive pass. The length of the pass often enabled the

fly-half to escape the clutches of the loose forwards, and made an important contribution to the development of such great fly-halves as Jackie Kyle, Cliff Morgan, Bev Risman, Richard Sharp and David Watkins, giving them extra time and space to use their skills to best advantage.

Ken Catchpole, the great Australian, made another significant contribution to the art of scrum-half passing. He was famous for his speed of pass from scrum, ruck, maul and lineout, and combined superb passing technique with tremendous agility and swift reactions. He was masterful in dealing with lineout ball, being able to get the ball accurately and quickly away from seemingly impossible situations. His superb technique and dexterity enabled him, seemingly in one movement, to receive, control and despatch any lineout deflection quickly and accurately to his fly-half. He often contacted the ball whilst it and he were both in mid-air, yet he was still able to fire a speedy, accurate pass. He became expert at dealing with the ball coming to him at different angles and at varying speeds and heights so, as well as making use of quality ball easily, more importantly he converted poor ball into good by his expertise.

Chris Laidlaw, the skilful New Zealander, introduced the spin pass to the international scene in the nineteen-sixties. His pass could send the ball great distances with speed and accuracy. Because Laidlaw played behind the great All Black pack he was able to fire it from a standing position. He not only delivered the pass with remarkable speed, control and accuracy, but off either foot and either hand. He became expert at getting into the right position to receive the ball, so that as little adjustment as possible was necessary before he made contact with the ball in his passing action.

Requirements of the scrum-half pass
All scrum-halves must have the basic ability to send out a stream of good passes. Haydn Tanner said of scrum-half passing: 'Each pass is a contest of speed versus length

versus accuracy.' Speed of thought, speed of action and speed of reaction are vital, and these come largely from a combination of co-ordination and agility. The knowledge of where and when to pass the ball will also contribute to the speed of pass as it will enable the scrum-half to make the necessary adjustments to his body position before he receives the ball. Then he can make the pass in one continuous movement immediately he makes contact with the ball. These adjustments in body position require good balance and quick footwork.

The scrum-half must also work on his strength and co-ordination to improve the length of his pass. The need for accuracy is obvious but cannot be overstated – ask any fly-half!

Every young scrum-half should try to become a two-sided player, capable of passing without delay from either foot and with either hand. Two-sidedness is an obvious advantage to a player in this pressure position, as it doubles his potential. Remember that you will be putting the ball in on the left-hand side of your scrummage, so the left-hand pass is an essential skill for a scrum-half.

The way in which a scrum-half makes a particular pass is determined by the possession he receives from his forwards, the time available and, most important, his body position relative to the ball and to the receiver. The pass may be delivered with or without spin from standing or with a dive.

The straight pass

This is the bread-and-butter pass of the scrum-half. It means that he has received the ball from his forwards in such a position that he can fire the pass immediately in one speedy movement, as he is able to see the ball, the receiver and the actions of his opponents. The position of the ball between him and the receiver makes it unnecessary for him to turn. The straight pass is the safest and quickest of passes, so the scrum-half should get into a position to use it wherever possible.

The standing pass allows the scrum-half more chance to be in a position to lend his support quickly to any attack. It has the further advantage of allowing him to alter his intentions if the pass is not 'on' for any reason: he may withhold the pass and run or kick, or he may even dummy and then run with the ball himself.

The dive pass may be used to make poor ball into good. The pick-up is made on the move and the ball may be contacted on the ground, near the ground or in the air. The pass is particularly suitable for dealing with a moving ball, for example when the forwards fail to control the ball properly. It should also be used when time is at a premium, for example under pressure from the opposing scrum-half particularly at your own put-in or when the ball is running loose. On wet days the dive pass may be used to scoop the ball away, and even in the dry it is usually a way of getting extra length to the pass.

The spin pass can be delivered from the standing position or from a dive. Because it is essentially a one-handed pass, the top hand being taken quickly across the ball to impart the spin, the scrum-half must practise with both hands so that he may spin the ball with either equally well.

The pivot pass

This pass is used on the many occasions during the game when the scrum-half receives the ball with his back to the receiver and so has to turn to pass the ball. The pick-up is

14 (*opposite, above*). The standing scrum-half pass: Clive Shell, playing for Wales v. Japan in 1973. Note the broad base, low body position, concentration on the target and follow-through. This excellent technique enables him to get the ball quickly away as he smoothly transfers his weight from left to right. He demonstrates the value of being a two-sided player, as he makes this pass – to what for most players is the more difficult side – look so easy and relaxed.

15 (*opposite, below*). The scrum-half dive pass: in this action from the Varsity match, the Oxford scrum-half displays good technique as he converts poorly controlled possession into 'good ball' by means of the dive pass. Despite the Cambridge pressure he concentrates on where he is passing as he gets the moving ball away.

from the front foot, which acts as a pivot as the passer turns. The eyes will obviously find the target much later than with the straight pass, and there is a greater risk of interception as the scrum-half is passing without being able to see the actions of his opponents.

The reverse pass

This pass, like the pivot pass, is used when the scrum-half needs to pass to a receiver who is behind him. It is a quicker pass than the pivot pass, but carries the same risk of interception and can be very erratic if not properly used and controlled. The pass is pushed or flicked under the armpit in the opposite direction to that in which the scrum-half is facing. The power comes from correct foot-placing, weight transfer, a smart push of the arms and a wristy flick. The head and shoulders should remain facing forward but the scrum-half can glance at the receiver.

Summary

The aim is a quick pass to the receiver which arrives with him at the right speed, the right length, the right place and the right time. This will only be achieved if you:

1. Pick up the ball from a broad base near the back foot for a standing pass.
2. Pick up from a narrow base near the front foot for a dive pass.
3. Know where the pass is going.
4. Know how the ball is likely to be delivered from the forwards.
5. Get into position quickly.
6. Keep your eyes on the ball as it comes to you.
7. Contact and pass the ball in one movement, with no hand adjustment and no backswing.
8. Keep your eyes on the target as you pass.
9. Stay low.
10. Transfer your weight.

THE KICKING SCRUM-HALF

In the art of tactical kicking, Clive Rowlands, the Welsh captain and coach of the 'sixties and 'seventies, was undoubtedly a master. The 'up and under' to the posts, the diagonal to the open-side wing and the chip into the box with either foot were all in his repertoire, but it was as a touch kicker that he could be relied upon to keep his team going forward. Under the old laws he was able to kick directly into touch from anywhere on the field and he had an uncanny skill in placing the ball just where he wanted it. Many held him and his brand of nine-man rugby responsible for stifling and smothering Welsh threequarter play, but all of Wales was happy when in 1963 he led Wales to their first victory over Scotland at Murrayfield for ten years. 'It was not an attractive match, and I felt sorry for the backs,' admitted Rowlands, 'but we were out to win and played to win. The pack did a great job.' Rowlands kicked the ball almost every time he received it and there were over 100 lineouts. The score was six points to nil including a Rowlands dropped goal – from a lineout.

There are many moments in a game when the scrum-half must choose to kick rather than pass and his kicking, like his passing, must have the essentials of speed, timing, accuracy and variety. He must understand the principles of kicking – hand hold, eyes on the ball, concentration and balance – and must work hard to master the punt, grub kick and drop kick with either foot.

Because it is so often performed under pressure, a scrum-half's kicking must be done quickly. He must be able to clear his lines from all types of seemingly impossible positions by using speed, agility and variations to find time and space to get an effective kick away with no danger of its being charged down. He must know how to shield the ball with his body by pivot kicking or kicking overhead, and both these techniques should be practised to improve speed and accuracy.

Despite the change in the touch-kicking laws, a

scrum-half who is given good quality position can still be an effective tactical kicker, and he should know how, where and, most important of all, why he is kicking. The considerations and options are similar to those which apply to kicking in attack, and these are discussed on pages 121–2.

THE RUNNING SCRUM-HALF

Sid Going, the former New Zealand scrum-half, was an outstanding exponent of the skills of the running scrum-half. Whether running as part of the tactical plan or as a result of his own initiative he caused problems for the best organised defences in the world. Going possessed all the skills of the natural runner – confidence, speed, strength, determination, sidestep and hand-off. At 5 foot 7 inches and 12 stones his speed off the mark made him extremely difficult to stop, whether he was breaking to score himself, initiating his own attacks or linking with his loose forwards. By providing a continual threat to his opponents he created more space for his outsides whenever he elected to serve them, as the opposing loose forwards' and half-backs' attention was focused upon him.

Britain has produced many fine examples of the running scrum-half over the years. As well as being great fifteen-a-side players they have often excelled in the seven-a-side game, where the extra space allowed them to show their skills to the best advantage. Players like John Williams (Harlequins, England and the Lions), Onllwyn Brace (Oxford University, Newport and Wales), Tremayne Rodd (London Scottish and Scotland) and Billy Hullin (Cardiff, London Welsh and Wales) all had that natural flair and gift for reading the game which enabled them to create openings which lesser mortals would never have seen, let alone made. Although different in physique and playing style, they shared the quick thinking to take advantage of any weak or hesitant defence, the knack of keeping their options open whilst putting their opponents in two minds, and the knowledge of when, why and how to run.

It is much easier to run when your team is going forwards, but like every other aspect of scrum-half play speed
of execution is vital. Run only when you have a chance of
success, usually when you have the element of surprise on
your side.

Breaking from the set scrum
Ideally these breaks should be made in conjunction with

16 The running scrum-half: Frenchman Roger Astre demonstrates a
natural gift for tactics as this quick heel against the head gives him an
opportunity to run from the scrum. He is certain to pose a threat as he
looks to see what is 'on' while he is accelerating away. He keeps his
options open for the developing situation by carrying the ball in both
hands.

the loose forwards, who will either set up the break or support the scrum-half break. Since the defence around the scrum will usually consist of two men on either side, conditions have to be very favourable before the scrum-half attempts an individual break, but moments will come when for one reason or another the defence is not alert. Recognising these moments is part of the scrum-half's tactical skill. They might occur:

1. On a quick heel, when the element of surprise is with you.
2. On a slow heel when your own scrum is driving the opposition backwards so that the defence is on its heels.
3. When the swing of the scrum has put the opposing back row temporarily out of the game.
4. When the opponents are temporarily short of a man, which generally means taking a man out of the back row.
5. When the opposing flank forwards are concentrating on your fly-half, and so are vulnerable to the dummy and run.
6. Against a weak tackler in the opposing back row.

On your own put-in, the normal break is coming round the back of the scrum after putting the ball in on the left, picking up the ball on the right of no. 8's feet and continuing down the right-hand side of the scrum. Alternatively, the pivot break involves picking up the ball and pivoting to run down the left of the scrum.

On your opponents' put-in, if your forwards heel against the head, the normal break will be down the left and the pivot down the right.

Breaking from the ruck or maul

Generally the opposing defence around the ruck or maul is one player either side. The scrum-half should always be aware of the possibility of this breaking down, particularly

108

when the ruck or maul penetrates into opposition territory. Look for situations where opposing players are tied
into the ruck or maul and you are going forward. If the ball
is won quickly, break in the same direction as the original
attack to stretch the opposition further. The scrum-half
should always be aware of the defence around the ruck or
maul and alert to exploit any weakness.

The dash for the line
However well the defence tries to mark, there are
moments when the scrum-half finds himself able to make a
dash for the line. This generally happens when your own
side is going forwards during scrummage, ruck or maul. The
dash is often just a strong dive preceded by a rapid, short-
paced run. The key factors are a quick pickup of the ball,
rapid acceleration, a low body position and a strong, determined dive. Everything about the dash must be explosive;
make your mind up quickly and run fast and aggressively.

In general, the scrum-half must be particularly alert
near the opponents' line, for any loose ball can lead to a
score. It is also important that he understands the law
which says that once the scrum, ruck or maul is on or over
the line it no longer exists. He is therefore legally allowed
to dive into the former scrum, ruck or maul to score a try.
A scrum-half who is awake and alive to these possibilities
often scores crucial tries for his team. Another possibility
to look for is the interception whenever your opponent is
forced to pass with his back to you to a receiver on your
side of the scrum (ie. to your right).

THE SCRUM-HALF AS COMMUNICATOR

Communication is essential to all successful team play, and
every side should have a code system which enables them
to perform planned movements and to communicate to
each other the direction of attack. All players should
be encouraged to help each other by calling helpful
instructions: it is a skill of the game which, if properly

used, can be highly effective, but like every skill it must be practised.

The scrum-half is a key person in passing on many of the team signals. It is particularly vital that the scrum-half and fly-half work out simple, clear signals in order to eliminate misunderstandings in communication. The scrum-half is also the 'eyes' of the forwards if their heads are buried in scrum, ruck or maul; he can see all round and should tell his pack what they should be doing.

Directional and tactical codes

From the fly-half's signal at the scrum or lineout the scrum-half knows in which direction he should pass. It should also be a guide to the direction in which the backs plan to attack, and the scrum-half passes the signal on to the forwards so that they know where to provide their support: on the short side, down the middle of the field or on the flank.

Conversely, if there is a planned move by the scrum-half and/or the forwards (a lineout peel or back-row pick-up from a set scrum, say), he transfers the information to his backs so that they may support the attack accordingly.

At short penalties the scrum-half relays the chosen tactic to the forwards as they get into position.

Lineout

The scrum-half receives the signal from the pack leader and relays it to the other forwards, particularly the thrower.

Set scrummage

The scrum-half should:

1. Ensure that the signals with his hooker are consistent and correct.
2. Help the forwards to communicate with each other, eg. calling for a wheel, eight-man shove or lock.
3. Tell the forwards when the ball is lost and out of the scrummage.

Ruck

The scrum-half should tell his forwards when the ball is on the ground. 'Walk it' or 'Feet' encourages them to drive over the ball.

Maul

The scrum-half must always identify for his forwards where the ball is and who has it. For example, 'On Dai, here left' will tell the forwards where best to apply their strength and expertise in the maul. Restraining arms and opponents who are preventing your side from winning good ball can often be removed thanks to simple words of encouragement and direction. The scrum-half may also encourage the forwards to start a drive by spinning off the maul with the ball.

Quality possession

If your pack has won the ball and is holding it safely in the back row of a scrum or in a maul, the forwards must be able to deliver it just when the scrum-half wants it, and not before. The key words from the scrum-half are 'Hold it' and 'Now'.

12

The Fly-Half

NATURAL REQUIREMENTS

Positional sense

A fly-half needs an outstanding positional sense above all else. Anyone who is expected to create opportunities for those around him has to understand the principles of time and space. Great fly-halves are able to find the best position to set up the attack and to dictate the rhythm and pace of the game.

Good positioning is at least sixty per cent a natural gift for reading the flow of the game. It enables a player to interpret instantly the movements of the ball carrier and to assess immediately and automatically the pattern of play which is likely to follow in the next few seconds. Only a computer can do this sort of calculation but to the gifted fly-half it is second nature. It has to be, for that is the only way he can think or see two or three moves ahead, defensively as well as in attack, and make the correct decision about when, where and how to start an attack or to take a more cautious position.

Imagination

The fly-half must play his game so that when he has the ball the opposition are always in two minds as to what he might do. They must be kept guessing and whenever possible taken by surprise. This built-in safety valve of imagination – with a touch of conservatism – means that a fly-half should never be caught at a loss when he has the ball. As the player who feeds and sparks those around him, he must be prepared either to inspire them with an imaginative move or to play safe in impossible situations.

Split vision

This ability to watch both the ball and the area around it allows the fly-half to read the play and to control the action. Since his main responsibility is to prepare the attack he must know what his players are doing, but he must also spot the best opening and put the ball there instantly. He must visualise the entire field and be aware not only of his own players' position but, possibly even more important, the positions of the opposing players.

TYPES OF FLY-HALF PLAY

Fly-halves come in different shapes: some are short and stocky; others are willowy and graceful; some are big and burly; others are slightly built. Though physical characteristics influence their style of play, they can be divided into three broad categories: those whose prime function is to scheme and to create openings for other players; those whose principal contribution is to run; and those whose major role is kicking. Of course, schemers should be able to finish off play when required and runners should be able to be constructive and creative when the situation demands it. All fly-halves should be able to kick well.

Which style a player adopts will naturally depend on his own strengths. Thus a fly-half may not be a particularly elusive or tricky runner yet possess a sound pair of hands and very good kicking ability. Or he may be weaker at kicking but more adept at running, jinking and side-stepping through the opposition's defensive lines. If you find a fly-half who combines all these qualities, hang on to him!

Few players have dominated their opponents as did Barry John, aptly nicknamed 'King John' after his exploits for the British Lions in New Zealand in 1971. We choose him as our model fly-half: he was a completely balanced player, able to pass well on either side, kick magnificently with either foot and break either way off either foot; in tactical awareness he was second to none and his supreme confidence in his own ability was an inspiration to other players in his team. He was also expert at punishing the mistakes of the opposition and at varying the game to suit the needs of his team. Whenever he received possession of the ball it was invariably used to good advantage.

The schemer and tactician

The fly-half who is a schemer and a tactician, capable of dictating play from midfield, is the backbone of the attack. Every great fly-half has a certain amount of this particular quality within him. Certain players like Jackie Kyle and Mike Gibson of Ireland, and currently John Bevan of Wales, show these qualities at their best. Their outstanding characteristic is the ease with which they handle the most difficult situations. This comes from their inspired positional awareness and uncanny ability to read the game instantly and truly. It is second nature to them to know when to part with the ball, which kind of pass or play is 'on' and which position to take up next. They always seem to be in the right place at the right time with minimum effort, and are artists at making the ball do the work.

The running fly-half

The jinker is the player who is full of exuberance and adds a dynamic touch to the game. He can fasten onto the ball anywhere and is fast and deceptive enough to burst through quickly to make a break or score. He is distinguished by his speed off the mark and by his jinking ability. Players such as Cliff Morgan, David Watkins and Phil Bennett of Wales, and Tom Brophy and Bev Risman of England, are fine examples of the jinking runner.

The slicer, on the other hand, relies on timing and sometimes physical strength and courage to get through the gap. Players such as Phil Horrocks-Taylor and Richard Sharp of England, Gordon Waddell of Scotland and Mike

English of Ireland were good examples of a slicing runner.

Whichever type of running fly-half you are, you need the ability to take on your opponent and beat him by swerve, sidestep or acceleration. Not only can a telling break make the difference between losing and winning a game; the fly-half can sometimes take the pressure off his team-mates by running at the opposition. All fly-halves should therefore learn the arts of faking and deceit by making feinting movements. The use of these fakes or feints will create more time and space either for the fly-half himself or for his colleagues. Fakes may be made with the eyes, hands, shoulders, body or legs, with or without the ball, and the object is to catch the opponent in two minds before taking the initiative. A clever player will develop his own faking moves. Faking skills may be used in defence as well as in attack, creating time and space to clear the line in tight situations.

Some of the more widely recognised fakes used by famous players are:

1. Deliberately slowing down before accelerating.
2. Moving one way before darting quickly the opposite way.
3. Looking in one direction before moving in the other.
4. Faking to pass and then running.
5. Faking to kick and then running.
6. Offering the ball before quickly pulling it back to move in the opposite direction.

The outside break. The value of this type of break is obvious. Once the opposing line is breached there is less defence to beat and, providing the support is quick and the passing is good, a score should result as the covering defence has little chance of getting to the man with the ball. A telling outside break can be devastating.

The inside break. This type of break is fraught with dangers. Indeed, it may well be part of the opposition's

115

plan to force the fly-half inside and thereby isolate him from his support. Also, once you step inside there is a tendency to continue with this action and you will end up among the opposing forwards. All the same, provided you realise the dangers of the inside break, you may use it to your advantage both in defence, to step inside the menace of a loose forward providing you are quick and agile at getting your kick away before it is charged down, and in attack. Here the inside break may be used against a flat threequarter line, particularly from a short pass taken on the burst at ruck or maul, or in the form of a quick swerve or sidestep to beat an opposing defender. John Bevan of Aberavon and Wales is an expert at this type of break against tight defences. John Bevan is also expert at linking effectively with his support and moving the ball away from the cover once the break is made. It is vital for a fly-half to realise that he must not only break but also link quickly to be effective.

The kicking fly-half

Every fly-half should be able to kick accurately with both feet to clear his line in defence or to give variety to the attack. Some fly-halves consciously choose kicking as the best tactic to set up their attacks; among those who have become famous (or infamous) at international level for their particular use of the boot are Alan Old of England and Barry McGann and Tony Ward of Ireland.

Like all other rugby skills, kicking needs practice, good judgement, precision in performance and a sound technique – eye on the ball, perfect balance, precision, accurate placement of the ball to the foot and a good follow-through. Kicking is like a golf swing, and timing is just as important. Similarly, the golfer knows which iron he will use to place the ball just where he wants it, and the accurate kicker must know which type of kick is needed at any one moment. He should have a mental picture of the position of the opposing full-back and the other backs, so that he can decide what kick to use and where to place it to gain a tactical advantage. In defence, the kicking fly-half's first priority is to find touch; the bouncing kick into touch may also be used further upfield to gain territorial advantage. In attack, his priorities are to place the ball where the opponents may be caught out of position, where they may be put under pressure, or where the ball can be regained quickly. His main weapons will be the chip kick, the grub kick and the up-and-under in attack, and the screw kick when going for a long touch.

THE FLY-HALF IN DEFENCE

The fly-half is an organiser in defence, bringing his three-quarter line up as quickly as possible to pressurise the opposing threequarter line. His own first priority is to ensure that his opposite number, or the player who takes the scrum-half's pass, does not make an outside break; the inside break should be dealt with by the back row. The second priority is to cover, both to support the full-back and wings and to be in a good position for a counterattack.

THE HALF-BACKS AS A TACTICAL UNIT

Communication and understanding

If scrum-half and fly-half can create a successful partnership based on ability, co-ordination and a sound system of communication, a good team will thrive on it. Each player should know intuitively what the other will do in any situation. This knowledge can only be achieved by time and practice, but once gained it will enable a pair of halves to dominate the opposition in their area of play and therefore to dominate tactics. It obviously helps if the pair has been playing together regularly for some time, but nothing takes the place of an efficient communication system of spoken, hand and feet signals. Some sort of signal should be passed at every lineout, scrum, ruck or maul if possible so that each knows what the other is going to do.

Half-back partners can also communicate by the

direction in which a player moves; his movement sparks off a pre-determined pattern of play. This also provides scope for 'false keys', as once an opponent has obviously discovered the pattern of the key, he can easily be misled by a false key, ie. a dummy run.

Variety

Variety is a strong tactic for half-backs. Too often play becomes stereotyped in similar situations during a game, when a little imagination and a variety of reactions would leave the opposition not knowing what to expect. The half-backs should practise to develop a range of skills and plays from similar game situations so that any movement chosen or forced on them during the game will come naturally to them.

For example, by varying the angle and distance at which they stand in relation to each other the half-backs may combine effectively to make it more difficult for their opponents to counter their moves. The fly-half may make use of the passing skills of his partner by varying:

1. His position relative to the opponents – shallow, deep, wide, near or behind.
2. How he takes the ball – running or standing still.
3. Where he takes the ball (ie. the angle of take) – straight or at different angles.
4. When he takes the ball – early or late.

Tactical appreciation

As the tactical pivot, the half-back pair must have a particularly well developed tactical sense. They must always:

1. Aim to play the ball over the gain line in such a way that it can be retained or regained and the support, continuity and pressure kept up.
2. Assess their own skill and confidence, and the quality of the ball being provided by their forwards, in the

light of the pressure being put upon them by the opposition.

3. Take into account the source of possession (scrum, lineout, etc.) and its position on the field.

Gareth Edwards and Barry John

Gareth Edwards and Barry John provided a shining example of a successful half-back partnership. Each player was capable of dominating tactics in his own way. They both possessed outstanding passing, handling, running and kicking skills. They seemed to play in complete harmony, always knowing what the other would do and reacting accordingly. As a result, each player could use his imagination and skills to the full for the benefit of the team.

13

The Backs in Attack

Backs do not take the field as mere spectators of an eight-a-side battle between two packs of forwards, but it is the possession and domination won by your forwards which usually decides your chances of success. There is, though, such an expression as 'Losing a game which we ought to have won', and it is quite possible for a team to provide itself with endless opportunities, yet turn none of them into an actual score, and then submit to the few chances gained by the opposition; we often read that a team's forwards gained good possession only for the backs to drop passes, give bad passes, kick unwisely or run into trouble. Although the reverse can also be true, and a limited amount of good possession provided by the forwards, say thirty per cent, can be made up for by excellent defensive work by your backs and the taking of the very limited opportunities presented to them, you would have to be very lucky to win with less than forty per cent good possession. Good possession in this sense is possession gained by the forwards (or even the backs in present times) from a scrum, lineout, ruck or maul which gives a team a chance to gain territorial or scoring advantage without immediate resistance from the opposition. It provides the opportunity to perform any pre-determined plan of attack, including set movements or ploys.

FIRST-PHASE BALL

Today's defences are so well organised that it has become

increasingly difficult to use a player's individual running talent from first-phase possession, ie. from scrum or lineout. Players are relying far more on using such talent from second-phase or third-phase possession.

This does not mean, though, that a player's natural gifts cannot be used on first-phase ball. For instance, going back to the example of a game plan which involves moving the ball away from a heavier pack for the benefit of a lighter, more mobile pack, there is nothing to stop a fly-half, centre or wing attempting a first-time break if he thinks it is at all possible, and the ball would still be moving away from the opposition pack and support should be close at hand. The scrum-half break might then be on from the resulting second-phase possession.

Another tactic involving quick movement of the ball could be for the backs to carry out a set ploy from first-phase possession, still taking the ball away from the opposition. The full-back making the extra man is a well-known one, and others are described on pages 128–39.

Kicking in attack (see page 122)
Tactical kicking to attack from first-phase possession can be used in two main ways:

The diagonal kick usually comes most effectively from your fly-half, over the opposing backs' heads and away from the opposing full-back. This gives your own three-quarters, particularly your open-side winger, a chance to reach the ball, supported by your back row, then your front five forwards. If the move is pre-determined the open-side winger will line up closer than usual to the gain line in order to save valuable yards.

The high kick, or *kick into the box*, landing behind the opposing pack, comes usually and most effectively from either the scrum-half or fly-half. It means that all the other team, except possibly the full-back, have to turn before chasing back after the ball. Your own team is already pointing and moving forwards, with a good chance of arriving at the second-phase ahead of the opposition.

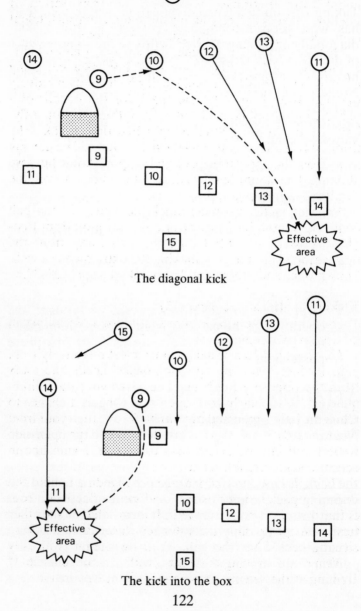

The diagonal kick

The kick into the box

SECOND-PHASE BALL

Taking first quite a common situation, where your team has won good second-phase possession after kicking diagonally or passing the ball swiftly to the wing, a switch of direction back the other way would find the opposition having to retrace their steps with little time for pause. Numerous channels can now be open to you. Assuming that it is not necessary to set up a third-phase ball, as the opposition is already disjointed and out of position at various points:

1. Any one of the attacking backs may find his path clear to make a clean break.
2. The ball could be fed to an overlapping player on either the open or the blind side.
3. The full-back could make an extra man, thus creating an overlap.
4. Any back could kick ahead to a completely un-marked space with the object of chasing and regain-ing possession.
5. A pre-determined set move could be brought into operation as the marking from the opposition might not be as close or as intense as from first-phase possession.

ATTACKING POSITIONS

Close to your opponents' try line
Near the touchline, blind-side moves involving the scrum-half, full-back and winger may be tried from lineout, scrum, ruck or maul. Alternatively, moves further along the back line might involve a quick change of direction or a dummying of change of direction. The idea of such moves is that you are so close to the opposing line that any slight hesitation by the opponents in making a tackle or reading a situation could well put you over for a score.

Near the posts, try either drop goals from the scrum-half, fly-half, centre or full-back, or again moves involving a quick change of direction or a dummying of a change of direction.

On your opponents' 22-metre line
Use similar moves to those for a position closer to the try line, but the opposition will probably be lying further away, particularly for a lineout, so moving the ball quickly away from the pack will give more room for set ploys and for the use of individual talent.

On halfway or your own 22-metre line
From halfway, similar moves to those described above are appropriate, but on your own 22-metre line you might be wiser to kick for position first. This kicking is not necessarily to touch, as long as the ball passes over the gain line to where one of your own team has an equal if not better chance of getting to it before the opposition. Bear in mind, too, that there is sometimes more room to start a running attack on your own 22-metre line.

Close to your own line
The prime tactic in this position is kicking up the touchline to gain territory and relieve pressure, but with particularly good ball and confidence on the part of all the backs this can be an ideal starting point for an attack. The initial movement of the ball would probably be across the field to get it away from the opposing pack. Combined with quick movement up the field and good support, this tactic has led to many tries.

ALIGNMENT AND COMMUNICATION

In attack a back line must almost always lie deep, or at a sharp angle from the scrum, lineout, ruck or maul, to give themselves room to carry out their movements.

A most important phrase, particularly among backs, is 'Yes, it's on', meaning perhaps that an overlap has been seen by the other player or players, but not by the ball

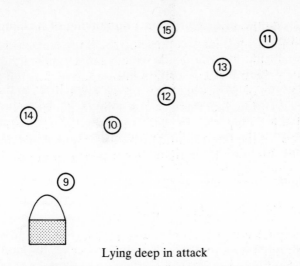

Lying deep in attack

carrier who is concentrating on taking and giving the pass. Give a team-mate the advice, 'Kick' when a pre-determined passing movement has been started but you can see that a quick kick might prove a better bet at that moment, for example if the ball carrier is about to be tackled in a bad defensive position.

THE FULL-BACK

The tactical part played by the full-back will depend on his particular attributes. Supposing the full-back is a competent kicker and safe tackler, but lacks both the initiative to join in threequarter movements and the running ability to counterattack after fielding a deeply kicked ball: in this case the coach, while encouraging the player to work on his vital running skills, will settle for a style of attacking back play which includes few moves involving the full-back.

On the other hand, if the full-back does have the aptitude for attack and counterattack it widens the scope of the threequarter line and indeed the whole team. In this case, however, greater responsibility for defence is placed on the whole threequarter line, particularly the wingers. For example, if a full-back comes into the threequarter line on the open side, the blind-side winger should make it his job to cover the full-back position in case the opposition take advantage of a mistake and break through to counter-attack. Although in this case the main responsibility is the blind-side winger's, in any situation in rugby every member of the team should be ready for a dropped or bad pass by his own team-mates from which the opposition may take advantage.

PLAYING TO THE FORWARDS

If your pack is bigger and heavier than the opposition's and your team's style of play is based on forward domination, your back's main role will be to support the back-row peels, scrum-half breaks and other moves which have been described in earlier chapters. When the ball does travel beyond the fly-half, the backs' main options are:

1. Kicking exceptionally high but not too far ahead so that your pack has time to get to the ball as it pitches (the 'up-and-under').
2. Kicking frequently down the touchline to set up line-outs from which further quality possession can be obtained.
3. Attempting moves such as those described on pages 140–3 which bring the ball back to the pack, then looking for support from your loose forwards and subsequently your other forwards. The aim is to carry the ball as far as possible towards your opponents' try line before setting up second-phase.

This style of play is commonly called 'ten-man rugby', the ten men being the pack plus the half-backs. Once domination has been achieved up front, both the opposition forwards and backs should be somewhat demoralised and the way should be open for the threequarters to use their talent and pre-determined ploys to take full advantage. Sometimes the attempted total domination up front meets such resistance that it is a slow process, in which case the threequarters can only be patient – sometimes, alas, until the final whistle.

14

Attacking Ploys in the Backs

Many set ploys or movements have been devised over the years and have proved successful for one team or another. To attempt an appraisal of them all would take a book in itself, so this chapter covers just some which have been used successfully over the last decade, with a suitable defence to each.

MOVES AWAY FROM THE FORWARDS

Missing the inside centre

The fly-half misses out the inside centre, passing straight to the outside centre, with the full-back making the extra man.

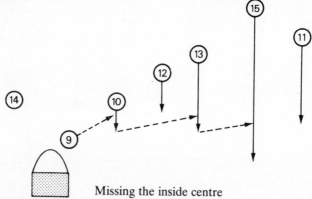

Missing the inside centre

Defence. The defending full-back comes forward to take his man, or the defending open-side winger comes in to tackle the full-back in possession.

Missing the outside centre

The inside centre misses out the outside centre, passing straight to the full-back making the extra man.

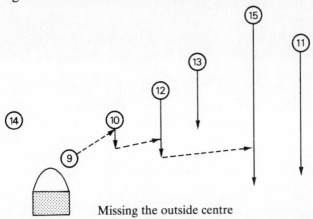

Missing the outside centre

Defence. Either as for the previous move, or the defending outside centre shuffles across to take the full-back.

Fly-half loop

The fly-half loops behind his inside centre, taking a return pass and thus making an extra man.

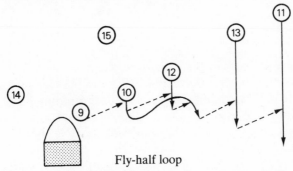

Fly-half loop

Defence. Depending on the team's system of defence for a scissors movement (see page 153), the defending inside centre could take the fly-half as he loops round while the defending fly-half takes the attacking inside centre.

Blind-side winger burst (1)

The fly-half loops behind his inside centre but does not receive a return pass. Instead the inside centre feeds his blind-side winger who is running hard through the original fly-half position.

Defence. The back-row forwards or defending fly-half should be in a position to tackle the winger.

Dummy scissors in the centre

The inside centre performs a dummy scissors with his outside centre, then feeds the full-back running hard onto the ball.

Defence. The defending outside centre should have stood his ground and thus be in a reasonable tackling position. Otherwise the defending open-side winger or full-back must take the attacking full-back.

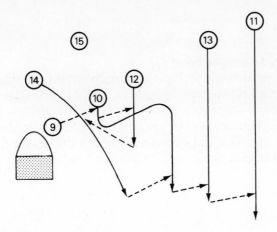

Blind-side winger burst (1)

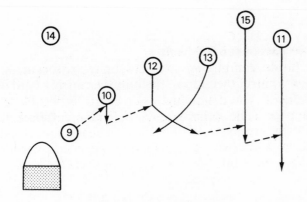

Dummy scissors in the centre

Open-side winger burst

The open-side winger, having hung back at first, runs hard between the two centres and takes a pass from the inside centre.

Defence. The defending outside centre is best placed to attempt a tackle. If he is unsuccessful it is up to the defending full-back.

Inside pass to the full-back

The full-back, running late between his two centres, receives an inside pass from the outside centre.

Defence. The defending inside centre is best placed to attempt a tackle, otherwise the defending full-back.

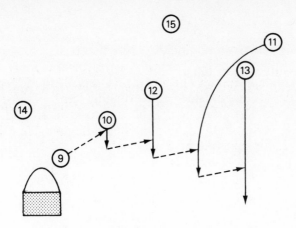

Open-side winger burst

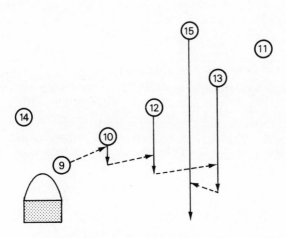

Inside pass to the full-back

133

Dummy scissors and outside centre burst

The scrum-half breaks laterally, performs a dummy scissors with his fly-half and his inside centre, then feeds a short pass to his outside centre running hard.

Defence. The inside centre, having stood his ground, can take the scrum-half, leaving the defending outside centre to tackle his opposite number.

Dummy scissors and outside centre miss

The fly-half performs a dummy scissors with the inside centre, then misses out the outside centre with a pass straight to the full-back making the extra man.

Defence. The outside centre shuffles quickly across to tackle the full-back, or the defending full-back or open-side winger makes the tackle.

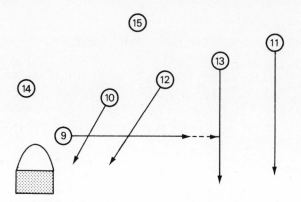

Dummy scissors and outside centre burst

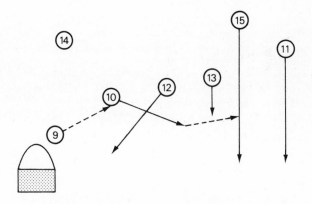

Dummy scissors and outside centre miss

Blind-side wing at fly-half

The blind-side winger takes the ball direct from the scrum-half on the open side, thus making the extra man.

Defence. The defending blind-side winger, back row or fly-half mark the winger and the rest of the defending backs shuffle across.

Blind-side winger burst (2)

The blind-side winger receives an inside pass from the fly-half, having run between the scrum-half and the fly-half, and attempts to break through the middle.

Defence. The defending back row, blind-side winger or fly-half take the winger and the rest of the backs shuffle across.

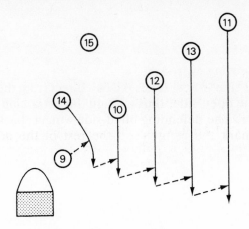

Blind-side winger at fly-half

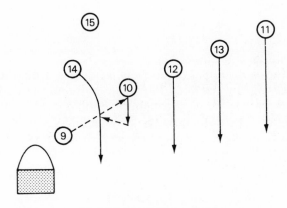

Blind-side winger burst (2)

Blind-side winger as extra centre

The blind-side winger joins the threequarter line outside the fly-half.

Defence. The defending blind-side winger, inside centre or back row should be suitably positioned to take the extra man.

Full-back on the blind side (1)

From a scrum, the scrum-half feeds the full-back on the blind side. The fly-half hangs back to cover any mistake.

Defence. The full-back should be tackled by the flanker, no. 8 or full-back. Or the defending blind-side winger can try a smother tackle.

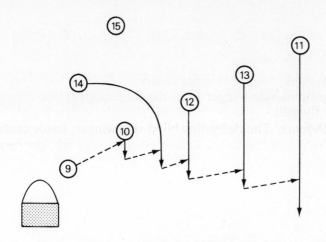

Blind-side winger as an extra centre

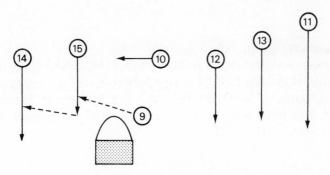

Full-back on the blind side (1)

Half-back scissors

The scrum-half runs laterally and performs a scissors with the fly-half.

Defence. The defending back row and fly-half are largely responsible.

Scissors further out

The outside centre loops back towards the pack behind the fly-half, taking a scissors pass from him.

Defence. The defending back row and the rest of the pack.

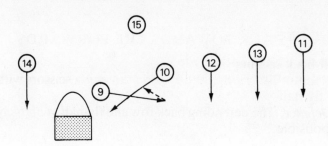

Half-back scissors

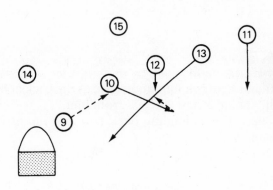

Scissors further out

Scissors with open-side wing
The open-side winger loops back behind his inside centre and takes a scissors pass from him.

Defence. The defending back row and fly-half should be suitably positioned.

Scissors in the centre
A scissors movement between the inside and outside centres.

Defence. The defending centres stand their ground and take each other's opposite number.

Scrum-half break
A break close to his pack by the attacking scrum-half.

Defence. The defending scrum-half and back row (see pages 67–8).

Kick into the box
The scrum-half or fly-half kicks back into the blind-side area. See diagram on page 122.

Defence. The blind-side winger or full-back should be suitably positioned to field the kick.

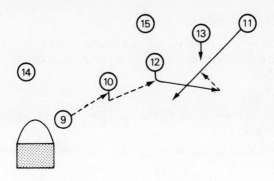

Scissors with the open-side wing

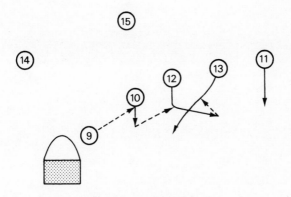

Scissors in the centre

MIDFIELD MOVES

These moves may be used from a scrum, ruck or maul on a line between the two sets of goal posts, ie. down the centre of the field.

Centre split
The centres split either side, and the scrum-half feeds the fly-half going to the left or right.

Defence. The defending opposite numbers and back-row forwards.

Full-back on the blind side (2)
Both centres and the fly-half line up on the same side, then the scrum-half feeds the full-back running down the other side. The fly-half hangs back to cover any mistake.

Defence. The defending full-back and back-row forwards.

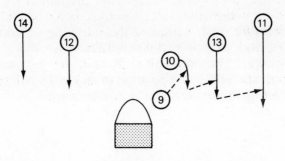

Centre split

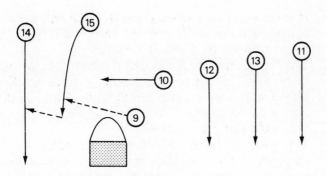

Full-back on the blind side (2)

Fly-half dummy run

The centres split either side, with the fly-half standing at one side with one centre. The fly-half makes a dummy run across the back of the scrum, but the ball is fed to the centre from the other side, who has crossed behind him to link with his other centre on the side from which the fly-half started. The fly-half moves first.

Defence. The defending fly-half, having stood his ground, should be in a position to tackle the ball carrying centre together with the back-row forwards.

SHORT PENALTY MOVES

The 'tap' penalty can be an extremely profitable source of penetrative attack, as many defences are not well organised against it. For a successful move from a 'tap' there must be good discipline and good organisation:

1. It must be clearly understood that the ball is to be collected quickly. This is the responsibility of the nearest player to it and of the scrum-half.
2. The captain must make a quick decision as to the ploy to be used, although occasionally a quick thinking player may take a quick tap to take advantage of a disorganised defence. In this case he will need immediate and sensible support.
3. The ploy to be used will vary according to the strengths of the team (fast-handling backs may opt to move the ball quickly, with the loose forwards giving support, whereas a strong pack may prefer to take on

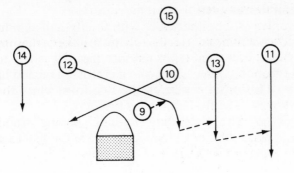

Fly-half dummy run

the opposition before releasing the ball) and on the position on the field at which the penalty has been awarded.

4. The team must form up at once in their pre-arranged positions, normally with the tight forwards on the short side and the backs on the open, with the loose forwards acting as supporters or runners according to the ploy which has been called.

Pivot moves

In recent years a number of pivot plays have been designed to confuse the defenders about which method of attack is to be used, and also to release the potential of powerful runners. Various attackers cross at speed behind a pivot player who usually has the opportunity of passing to one of three players. His team-mates know which player is going to receive the ball and organise their support accordingly. Clear signals and good timing are essential.

Some examples of pivot moves are:

1. The scrum-half feeds the pivot, then runs round behind him and takes a return pass.

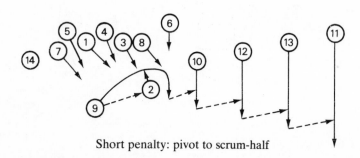

Short penalty: pivot to scrum-half

2. The scrum-half feeds the pivot and runs round behind him on a dummy run, while the ball is fed to a centre who has crossed behind the pivot and who will link up with the forwards on the blind side.

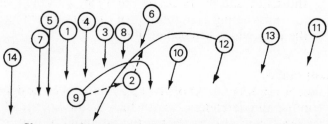

Short penalty: pivot to centre, scrum-half on dummy run

3. Similar to the previous move, but the centre also makes a dummy run and the ball goes from the pivot to a third player, usually a big, strong runner, who

takes it running close to the pivot and towards the open side.

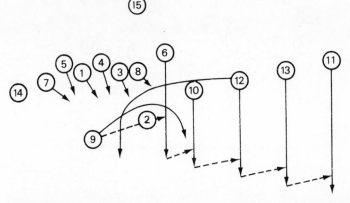

Short penalty: pivot to forward, scrum-half and centre on dummy runs

Other moves

1. The scrum-half gives a normal pass from the tap to his fly-half, who starts a conventional back movement.
2. The scrum-half feeds the fly-half standing on the open side, who feeds the ball back to his forwards on the blind side.

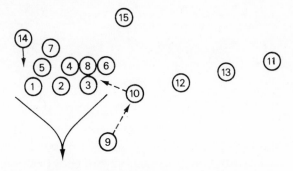

Short penalty: the fly-half passes back to his forwards

149

3. The scrum-half runs laterally, performing a dummy scissors with his fly-half but a scissors with either the inside or the outside centre.

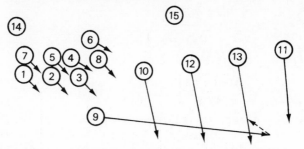

Short penalty: dummy scissors by the scrum-half

15

The Backs in Defence

The importance of a positive attitude to the game has already been emphasised. This attitude is founded largely on your confidence in your ability to attack the opposition, but at the same time it would clearly be very unwise to ignore altogether the preparation and organisation of your defence. Indeed, part of a team's positive attitude is the players' confidence in their ability to defend their line against the variety of attacks the opposition will throw at them.

There are many channels and aspects of attack, but defence can be built largely round two factors: the ability to read a situation, and effective tackling. No matter what defensive plan you may adopt, however rigid or flexible, it depends primarily upon the tackling ability of your team in relation to the running ability of your opponents.

This does not mean, though, that a defensive plan may as well be disregarded if one or two members of the team are poor tacklers. What it does mean is that any attacking plan by your opponents, however well organised, will usually be open to failure if counteracted by good defensive positioning and by good tackling.

DEFENCE AGAINST SPECIFIC TACTICS

In defence as in attack, organisation and pre-determined plans play a vital part: and in defence as in attack, those plans will depend primarily on your coach's assessment of the relative strengths and weaknesses of the two teams. If, for example, your opponents are likely to field a fast-running, quick-handling threequarter line, then your threequarters must be alerted to play a large part in your defensive plan. However, if they are more likely to play ten-man rugby to their forward strength, then your inside backs, full-back and blind-side wingers can expect to be the points of attack.

If facing the first, more fluid style of play your coach would encourage quickness up into the tackle, to get in amongst their threequarter line smartly, to break down the flow of the ball and so to gain possession of it yourselves. If you achieve this the opposition has to search for other channels of attack which might not be so suitable for the talents and ability within their team.

Against the second style of play, that of forward domination, your coach should prepare the threequarters, particularly the inside backs, full-back and wings, for an initial period of heavy tackling and of catching high and hanging kicks. If these players stand up well to this pressure, once again the opposition may have to look for other methods of attack less suitable to their strengths.

DEFENCE AGAINST SET PLOYS

See also the previous chapter, pages 128–50.

Extra man in the line

If an opposing full-back comes into the line from either first-phase or second-phase ball, who marks him? There are two options: either the defending full-back specifically takes his own man, wherever he enters the line, be it between or outside the centres, or even outside the wing; or each threequarter tackles the man immediately in front of him. For example, if the full-back was entering the line outside the centres the defending winger could confront him and leave his opposing winger to the defending full-back.

Similarly, to counter scissors, dummy scissors, loops,

dummy runs, miss movements etc, the two alternatives are either for each defending back to take his opposite number or for each defending back to tackle the player who ends up in front of him. To illustrate that these are not necessarily the same, take the example of the attacking fly-half looping behind his inside centre for a return pass. The defending fly-half either follows him round and continues to mark him, or he tackles the attacking inside centre, leaving his own inside centre to take the attacking fly-half.

Overlaps

What about opponents' attacking movements involving an extra man, when by coming up too obviously into the defensive line your full-back might leave you very exposed to the kick ahead or when for some other reason you find yourself with, say three defenders against four attackers or two against three? The answer to any overlapping attack is what is called 'shuffling across'. The defending three-quarter line, particularly the centres, anticipate the full movement of the ball across the field and so do not fully commit themselves to tackling their opposite numbers. Once their opposite numbers, under the impression they are going to be tackled, have passed the ball the defenders move quickly, or shuffle, across the field in an attempt to tackle the next man with the ball. This relies on a lot of tactical appreciation and on the quick reading of a situation; if it is badly performed it can open a defensive gap.

An additional defensive tactic is to entice the opposition into doing what you want them to do. You might encourage the attacking ball carrier to attempt a break himself by deliberately showing him a gap, but then tackle him with the ball as he goes for it; or you might rush up quickly and pressure him to hurry his pass or kick.

Short penalties

If a penalty is awarded against you, keep your eyes on your opponents as you retreat the statutory ten metres. If there is time, the defence must be organised both to take the first

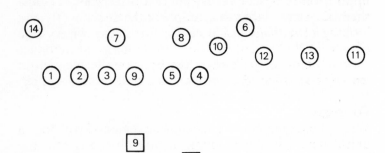

Defence against the short penalty

tackle and to have some depth in case the first tackle is beaten; the exact organisation will depend on the tackling skills of the forwards. The easiest way is for the front row to take the short side, the locks and scrum-half to mark the tap and the pivot, and the loose forwards and backs to mark the open side. Either one player (normally a forward) can rush the ball carrier or pivot, hoping to catch him in possession, or the defensive line can move forward at a slower pace, thus giving the opposition time to complete their ploy, but then tackle the resultant ball carrier.

DEFENCE AGAINST KICKS

Attacking kicks from your opposition can be a problem if not dealt with in an organised way. The men concerned here are primarily the full-back and both wings. The player in the best position to catch the ball should take it, having called clearly. Usually it is the player in whose direction the ball is coming who is best placed to catch it, but a player running forwards towards the ball is also in a good position to take it.

A kick into the box should be dealt with by the blind-

154

side winger or the full-back. If the full-back is standing wide, the blind-side winger should be better placed for the kick. If the full-back is more orthodoxly positioned on a line with the set piece or the opposing half-backs, he would then be better placed to catch the ball.

A high, midfield kick should nearly always be the full-back's.

A diagonal kick can be either the open-side winger's or the full-back's, depending on the positional role of the full-back and also on who arrives at the ball first.

ALIGNMENT

In defence a threequarter line must lie up flat, as close as possible to the gain line without getting off-side. This gives the opposition as little time as possible to pass, kick or run with the ball.

SUPPORT

Most teams in these days of the 'extra man' ploy virtually use two full-backs at set pieces. In other words the full-back stands wider to cover kicks and overlapping movements on the open side, and the blind-side winger stands farther back and closer to the touchline to deal with kicks or movements back to his side of the field. Whenever a ball is kicked ahead by the opposition, all the threequarters at least should make the effort to get back as quickly as possible with their full-back or winger in order to give him support and more scope for counterattack. In fact, the backs should be continually supporting one another. Supposing, for example, that their powerful centre is obviously making a definite attempt to run through one of your centres, the defending fellow centre could well leave his opposite number to help in tackling his team-mate's opponent. This being the case, both must do all in their power to prevent him from feeding the ball.

Similarly, if a winger is confronted by a very quick

opponent, the inside players of his team (the centres and full-back) should bottle up the option of that player coming inside his man. The defending winger then has to face only the options of the attacking player trying to go outside him or kicking ahead.

Important though support in defence is, the best defence of all is good, strong, man-to-man tackling.

COMMUNICATION IN DEFENCE

Definite calling for the ball is a must and every player in the team should be encouraged to shout 'My ball' when he intends to catch the ball from a high kick. When a ball might well be fielded by either one of two players, the first player calling should be given the opportunity to catch it, but the other player must be ready to help if his team-mate fumbles or drops the ball or is even caught in possession.

Often in defence, you will hear the words 'OK, I've got him', which means that another player, although an opponent is his responsibility, can turn his attention to the next opponent in the knowledge that the first man is covered by the team-mate who made the call. Or there is the shout of 'Plenty of time' to a team-mate who is running back to gather a kick ahead by the opposition without knowing how close the opposition are to bearing down on him.

16

Counterattack

In essence, counterattack is changing a defensive situation into an attacking one. Its greatest value is that during the quick transfer of the ball between teams, the team that loses possession has not time to organise its defence. Thus the counterattacking team often receives the ball in space and with time. If they move quickly they may have the advantage of broken play when defences are less organised and where their running and handling skills are not limited by any strong defensive line or cover from the opposition.

Counterattacking has always been part of the game. Higham and Higham, back in 1960, said that counterattack 'Means not only getting your man, but getting the ball; it means not only stopping but forcing him back; it means being first up after the tackle to take the ball on, or going on a loose ball only with the intention of getting up with the ball in your hands. In other words, defence is a matter of not only stopping an attack but starting a counterattack.' Since then two important changes to the laws have increased the opportunities for counterattack. First, a player no longer has to play the ball with his foot after the tackle; and second, a player may no longer kick the ball directly into touch from outside his own 22-metre line, except from a penalty.

Another important fact is that rugby is not only a running, handling, kicking game but also a game where a great number of mistakes occur. A lively and alert side will always take advantage of the counterattack possibilities presented by their opponents' mistakes, whether these are made from pressure, lack of concentration, breakdown of skill, or misunderstanding or hesitation between players.

WHEN TO COUNTERATTACK

It is important to recognise the situations from which a counterattack may work. These are mainly:

1. After an opposing player has been tackled and the ball has run loose.
2. When the ball has run loose from a scrum, lineout, ruck or maul, or in general play.
3. From a kick-off or drop-out by the opposition which has gone too far or from which a good catch has been made.
4. From a penalty kick at goal or to touch.
5. From a misdirected or poorly supported punt into the box or downfield.
6. From a dropped or intercepted pass by the opposition.
7. After a quick restart (eg. short penalty, lineout, drop-out) by your own side.

ESSENTIALS OF COUNTERATTACK

Confidence is the key. Players must believe in their own ability, and that of the team, to take on the opposition. Practice will bring this confidence.

Judgement is needed to assess not only whether the opposition might be vulnerable to a counterattack but also the quality of your own support.

Speed is vital. The quicker the ball is moved the less time the defence has to reorganise.

Support the player and the ball. For example, if a full-back fields a long punt downfield, players must run back to get behind him if he is not to be left stranded. There should be a number of receiving points to which the first pass may be made, and players must learn these positions and get to

158

them quickly so that there is no loss of time in getting the counterattack under way.

Imagination is an invaluable asset, since if the conditions are right a counterattack can be initiated from anywhere on the field. Obviously, the nearer you are to your own goal line the greater the element of risk.

Attack the opposition at its weakest point, for example by moving the ball quickly to the side of the field where your team-mates outnumber the opposition. If there is no obvious point, try to create one with a scissors or a similar rapid change of direction.

PRACTISING COUNTERATTACK

Players' confidence and tactical appreciation of counter-attack possibilities can be improved by constant practice and coaching. For example, using one half of the field only, a full threequarter line can form up as if receiving a kick-off. Then, depending on the ability of the players and the stage of their coaching, three, five or even seven other players can kick the ball towards them and to any position in the field of play. The threequarter line then attempts to counterattack in the best way possible.

Alternatively, two players can kick towards three or four players in a smaller area, giving them the chance to counterattack using their superior numbers.

EXAMPLES OF COUNTERATTACK

In 1966–67 London Welsh adopted counterattack as its main principle of play. The side at that time had very few big forwards, so primary possession was hard to come by. We always had to pressure the opposition and counter-attack. We were a side, in fact, that lived off any ball we could win by our pressure defence. The team tackled, tackled and kept on tackling, and many famous victories were achieved during that season, seemingly against the odds; the key to those victories was the counterattack.

Many famous and exciting tries have been scored by counterattack, but perhaps in recent times the most famous and most fascinating was that started by Phil Bennett while playing for the Barbarians against the All Blacks in 1973. He initiated the counterattack deep inside his own 22-metre area with a series of sidesteps. He then passed the ball to his supports who carried it forward to enable Gareth Edwards to score a try which will always be remembered as one of the greatest in the history of rugby. There have been many accounts of this famous try and it was an object lesson in counterattack. The key factors were:

1. The change of possession (Bryan Williams' kick into the 22-metre area).
2. The imagination of Phil Bennett to launch the counterattack.
3. The speed of his sidesteps.
4. The immediate support and re-alignment; four players handled the ball within thirty metres of their own line.
5. Confidence and judgement of all the players involved in the movement.

This try showed that when executed properly, counterattack is the showpiece of the game. All successful sides should work to improve this exciting aspect of team play.

17

Re-Starts and Free Kicks

KICK-OFF FROM HALFWAY

Kicking side

The normal tactic is to kick the ball to drop on the inter-section of the ten-metre line and five-metre line. It should be high enough for your forwards to arrive at the same time as the opposition. Your forwards then drive in quickly to get possession: either your locks win the ball by jumping for it while it is still in the air, or the tacklers win it by putting the receiver on the floor or by turning him for their team-mates.

Alternatives include the kick away from the forwards, either for your own open-side winger to set up an attack, or for touch near the opponents' corner flag on either side of the field, or deep towards their posts to force a drop-out or kick for touch which will give your side the advantage of a throw at the lineout.

Receiving side

The defending forwards, who will have lined up roughly in scrum formation, must support the catcher so that he has the option of finding touch, making a mark or driving forward before slipping the ball back to his support.

The inside centre and open-side winger position them-selves about halfway between the 22-metre and ten-metre lines, the open-side winger being right on his touchline. The outside centre is further back, on or near the 22-metre line to deal with a long kick-off to the open side. The full-back and blind-side wing take up positions about ten

161

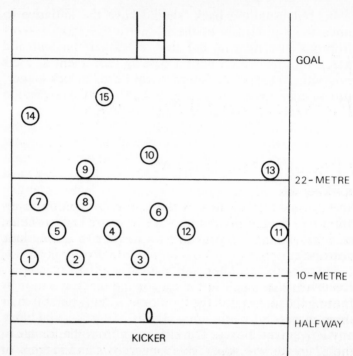

GOAL

22-METRE

10-METRE

HALFWAY

KICKER

Defence at the kick-off

metres from the try line, the full-back nearer his goal posts, the blind-side winger nearer the touchline. The scrum-half is directly behind his forwards, with the fly-half suitably positioned infield. By adopting this formation the threequarters are well placed to deal with any form of unconventional kick. It would be very difficult for the opposition to get to any ball, whether kicked short or long, before the defending team. Players should always be alert to deal with any variety of kick, particularly the full-back, outside centre and open-side winger.

22-METRE DROP-OUT

Kicking side

Always try first a quick drop kick. Any member of the

162

team, but usually a back, should have the initiative to move the ball swiftly to the 22-metre line, take a short drop-out just clearing the line, re-gather the ball and attack the opposition with a passing movement at their most vulnerable point. Alternatively he might kick longer, into an open space, and chase the ball to regain possession deep in opposition territory.

If this tactic is successfully blocked by the opposition, you will usually have to resort to the more formal drop-out using your specialist kicker to put the ball in front of your forwards as for a kick-off from halfway. The kicker must still keep his eyes open for any weaknesses in the defensive line-up and exploit them, for example by kicking to his blind-side wing or by dummying to take an ordinary kick and then taking a short tap over the line or a long kick downfield.

Receiving side (see page 164)

If the opposition take a quick drop-out the nearest two or three players must attempt to harrass the kicker and block any movement. For a normal drop-out from the centre of the 22-metre line, two forwards usually stand in front of the kicker, attempting to block his kick, while the other forwards stand opposite the kicking side's pack. This leaves the threequarters to cover other areas of the field.

The open-side winger should stand near the touchline and just outside the 22-metre line, one centre taking up a similar position but twenty yards behind the winger. The other centre is about twenty yards in front of the kicker, towards the open side. The full-back is about forty yards in front of the kicker, while the blind-side winger and scrum-half should be behind the forwards with the fly-half suitably positioned infield. Once again all the space is covered and the team dropping out would find it very difficult to gain possession of the ball first.

The player who actually catches the ball has the same options as the receiver of the ball from a kick-off (see page 161).

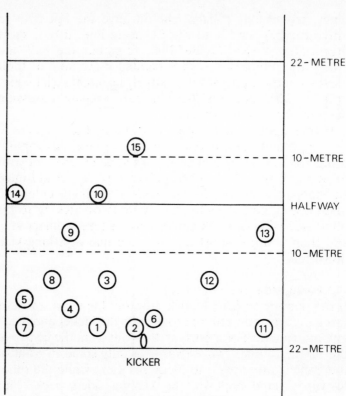

Defence at the 22-metre drop-out

PENALTIES AND FREE KICKS

For the section on short penalties see pages 146–50.

The kick for touch

The defending side must retire ten metres as soon as a penalty is awarded, keeping the opposition in full view all the time. If it is clear that they are going to kick for touch you must take up a suitable formation: immediately behind the forwards, on the touchline, will be your blind-side winger and behind him your full-back. Your centres and open-side winger will be in normal alignment across the

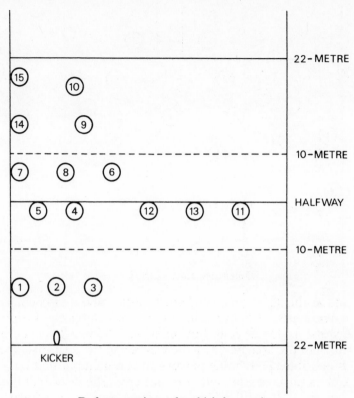

Defence against a free kick for touch

field with your scrum-half and fly-half supporting your blind-side winger and full-back who are the players most likely to field a missed touch-kick unless it is badly sliced.

The attacking side should follow the kick in a more or less orthodox line formation, marking man for man, but the full-back should hang back.

The kick for goal
The defending side knows, once the opposition has elected to kick at goal from a penalty decision, that the ball must be propelled a visible distance from the mark. This means that they should have good time to organise themselves

165

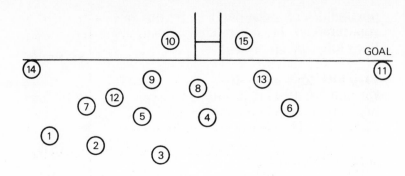

Defence against a kick for goal

and at the same time not have to worry about tap penalty movements. It is difficult to give a set defensive system against a kick at goal, but the general idea is to cover as much of the area between the kicker and the dead-ball line as possible. Defending players must remember that if the kick is unsuccessful and does not cross the dead-ball line then the ball is still in play. They can either touch it down if it crosses the try line or counterattack, preferably by working one side of the field and then switching, or kick for touch. Good catchers must be positioned in front of the posts for any attempt at goal which falls short.

The attacking side must follow up sensibly and swiftly to give the defenders as little time and room as possible to counterattack or to attempt a clearing kick. There is also the possibility of the ball striking a post and rebounding into play, giving the attacking team the greater element of surprise. Usually your quickest runner, probably a winger, chases towards the posts in the hope of gaining possession or catching an opposing player in possession. The full-back and the other winger can hang back slightly to cover the

166

possibilities of a clearing kick by the opposition or of a counterattack breaking through their team-mates who have followed up the kick.

Free kick from a penalty

Certain offences are penalised by a free kick, which does not permit a direct attempt at goal. If the team awarded the kick is in defence, well in its own half, the tactical approach has changed very little and the kick to touch is still the favourite ploy.

However, if your side is awarded a free kick much closer to your opponents' line, other options are open to you:

1. Finding touch close to your opponents' corner flag – assuming your forwards are winning a fair share of lineout ball.
2. A tap penalty using any of the ploys already described.
3. A tap penalty, followed by an attempted drop at goal. Either the kicker may take the tap himself, or he may have the ball passed to where he is standing in a favourable kicking position.

Index

half-backs 117–18; between backs 124–5, 156
compression 80
concentration 35
contact 14, 82–3, *see also* tackling
counterattack: defined 157; opportunities for 158; examples of 159–60
Crauste, Michel 47
Craven, Danie 99
cross kicks 13
cup competitions 2

Dauga, Benoit 46
Davies, Gerald 14, 37, 85, 87
Davies, Mervyn 25, 26, 46, 47, 72, 73, 76
defensive kicks 13
deflecting 70, 75–6
determination 35, 42
diagonal kicks 18, 29, 122
dive pass 99, 103
Dixon, Peter 45, 46, 87
drop kick 162–3
du Plessis, Morne 26, 46
dummy pass 13, 38
dummy scissors 78, 130–1, 134, 150, 152

Edwards, Gareth 98, 99, 119, 160
eight-man shove 15, 64–5
Ellis, Jan 45, 47
England 26
English, Mike 114–15
equipment 10
Evans, Geoff xv
Evans, Trevor 46
extra man 152–3, 155

Faking 115
fitness: and rota system 6; training for 10, 11–12, 17; of opponents 27–8; in forwards 40, 43
flankers: as captains 26; right and left 43–5, 47; in scrum 52, 54, 56, 61–3, 65–9; as throwers 71
floodlighting 6, 9
fly-halves: and team strategy 20; as captains 26; and tactical appreciation 37; and attack from set scrum 60–1; and defence at set scrum 64–8;

British Lions' 100; natural requirements of 112–13; as tacticians 114, 117–19; running by 114–16; kicking by 116; in half-back partnership 117–19; in set movements 128–31
foot positioning 13, 15, 54–6
forwards: training of 14, 16; and team strategy 18–19; as captains 26; role of 40, 81; characteristics of front 40–1; role of loose 41–2, 43–4, 45–7; counters to opposition's strengths 48–9; position in set scrum 56–7, 65; tactics in set scrum 60–3; position in lineout peel 77–8; and contact skills 83; and rucks 88–9; and kick-off 161
Fouroux, Jacques 26
France 26, 37, 47, 72, 76, 107
front five 40–1
full-backs: and team strategy 20; as captains 25–6; speed of 28; and pitch conditions 30; and tactical appreciation 37–8; tactical role of 125–7; and defence at kick-off 161–2

Gain line 58, 59
garryowen 13, 31, 89
Gibson, Mike 39, 114
goals 29, 33, 123, 165–6
Going, Sid 50, 96, 99, 106
Goodall, K. G. 46
Gourdon, Jean François 37
Gray, Tony 47, 71
Greyling, Piet 46, 47
grids 10
grub kick 13, 37, 105, 117

Hands: position of when kicking 13; and deflection 70
half-backs: and pitch conditions 29–31; as tactical unit 23, 117–19
handling 11, 14
Harlequins 52, 106
Higham, E. S. and W. J. 157
Hipwell, John 26
hookers 51, 55, 56–9, 71
Hopwood, D. J. 46
Horgan, Denis xv
Horrocks-Taylor, Phil 114
Howcroft, Chris 74
Hullin, Billy 106

pivot moves 147–9
pivot pass 99, 103–4
Pontypool 52, 90
possession: training for 11; second-phase 18, 32, 123; at lineout 70; and scrum-half 97, 111; first-phase 120–1
Powell, Ed 74
press reports 27
pressure 35–6
Price, Graham 95
progression, in training 12
props 40, 41, 51, 52–6, 65

Quinnell, Derek 45, 46, 82, 95

Ralston, Chris 74, 75
referees 89, 91, 94
regularity, in training 12
reverse pass 104
Richmond 74
Risman, Bev 100, 114
Rives, Jean-Pierre 47
Rodd, Tremayne 106
Rogers, Budge 46
Rowlands, Clive 99, 105
rucks: training for 10, 16–17; and loose forwards 43, 44, 81; and leaning 83; technique of 87–9; tactics at 94–6; breaking from 108–9; signals in 111
rugby football: changes over last decade in 2, 7; mini- 2, 3, 10; clubs 2–6; schools 4; sevens 106
rules, changes in 7, 70, 97, 105, 157
running: training 13–14; and scrum-half 106–9; and fly-half 114–16

Scanning 14
schoolboy rugby 2, 4, 10
scissors 140–2, 150, 152, *see also* dummy scissors
Scotland 26, 105, 106
screw kick 13, 117
scrum(s): training for 10, 15, 16; kicking to obtain 18; and forwards 40, 44; domination of 48–9; improved by practice 50; psychological impact of 50; binding of 51–4; foot positions in 54–6; body positions in 56–7; channelling ball from 57–8; attack

from set 59–64; defence at set 64–9; spinning 65–6; breaking from set 107–8; signals in 110
scrum-halves: and team strategy 19–20; as captains 26; and co-ordination of put-in 59; and attack from set scrum 60–3; and defence at set scrum 65–9; and throwing 73–6; and shortened lineout 78; and rucks 87; 94–6; and mauls 91–2, 94–6; qualities required in 97–8; British Lions' 99; passing 99–104; kicking by 105–6; running by 106–7; breaking by 107–8; as communicator 109–11; in half-back partnership 117–19; in pivot moves 148–9
scrummage machines 10
second-phase possession 18, 32
selection 8, 21–3, 71
seven-a-side rugby 106
Sharp, Richard 100, 114
Shell, Clive 103
short penalties: moves for 146–50; defence against 153–4
sidestep 13, 19
signals 23, 110, 117
size: of pitch 29; of players 43, 45, 47
Skrela, Jean-Claude 47
Slattery, Fergus 45, 46, 47
slicing 114–15
slope, of pitch 29
snap shove 15
South Africa 26, 45–7, 99
Spanghero, Walter 46
specificity, in training 12
speed 17, 43
spin pass 97, 99, 100, 103
Springboks 45–7, 99
squad(s) 5–6, 19
Squire, Jeff 52, 95
stamina 17
standing pass 103
strategy: definition of 1; determination of 2, 6, 18; coaching of 11, 25; and available talent 18–21
strength 17
Stuart, R. 46
studs 30
sun 30
sweepers 31